Badass
STORIES

Badass
STORIES

GRIT, GROWTH, HOPE,
AND HEALING
IN THE SH*TSHOW

JODIE ECKLEBERRY-HUNT, PH.D., A.B.P.P.

TURNER
PUBLISHING COMPANY

TURNER PUBLISHING COMPANY
Nashville, Tennessee
www.turnerpublishing.com

Badass Stories: Grit, Growth, Hope, and Healing in the Sh*tshow

Cover and book design by William Ruoto

Library of Congress Cataloging-in-Publication Data

Names: Eckleberry-Hunt, Jodie, author.
Title: Badass stories of grit, growth, hope, and healing that inspire the
   hell out of me / Jodie Eckleberry-Hunt, PhD, ABPP.
Description: Nashville, Tennessee : Turner Publishing, [2023] | Includes
   bibliographical references.
Identifiers: LCCN 2022013259 (print) | LCCN 2022013260 (ebook) | ISBN
   9781684429127 (paperback) | ISBN 9781684429134 (hardcover) | ISBN
   9781684429141 (epub)
Subjects: LCSH: Determination (Personality trait) | Resilience (Personality
   trait)
Classification: LCC BF698.35.D48 E47 2023 (print) | LCC BF698.35.D48
   (ebook) | DDC 155.2/32--dc23/eng/20220914
LC record available at https://lccn.loc.gov/2022013259
LC ebook record available at https://lccn.loc.gov/2022013260

Printed in the United States of America

To all those living in the shitshow alongside me.

Contents

. . .

HOPE

HEALING

Introduction

. . .

Have you ever really wanted to do something but let fear get in the way? Did the desire persist and linger in the back of your mind until you finally did something about it?

I really wanted to write a book like this back in 2002. I wanted to call it *What Advice Do You Have for Someone Like Me?*

Fear got in the way—but grit won out in the end.

As I begin, let me share my story.

Early in my career, I worked with a lot of older folks in hospitals and medical clinics. They were in vulnerable positions, and I'm certain they weren't excited about seeing a naïve, cheerful young psychologist.

I would introduce myself and ask this question to break the ice: "What advice do you have for someone like me?" My intent was to communicate respect and a desire to listen. I wanted to help the people feel more at ease. Paradoxically, however, I found that I was the one who was likely helped the most by the answers I received.

The advice folks shared was profound, and it was always

directly related to their current struggle. People would start by offering a nugget of advice, but then they would tell me a story—a story with healing properties—powerfully layered with meaning. They were badass stories. Kick-ass stories.

I love narratives, and I began to get excited about the next inspirational tale I'd hear in response to my question. Back in 2002, I thought to myself, *I have so many stories. I want to write a book about them*, yet I didn't write a thing. I got busy, and life proceeded.

Years later, I told some friends how much I loved reading Rachel Naomi Remen's *Kitchen Table Wisdom*,[1] a book of short, healing narratives. Remen's writing was poignant and eloquent. Her style made me feel all warm inside, like curling up with a blanket and cup of hot cocoa and giving myself a hug. While I was immersed in her prose, I felt whole because healing was seemingly available no matter how big the screwup. It was all in the way you looked at the situation.

When I conjured an image of kitchen table wisdom, I saw people connecting in a relaxed setting, with stories of experience, survival, and advice in a comfortable space. The title conveyed a sense of closeness and bonding. I imagined a group of people sharing and mentoring. Everyone would have something to contribute. Everyone would be accepted. There would be tears and hugs.

I love that shit—at least in theory.

I say "in theory" because while the idea of folks bonding in the kitchen looks good in the movies, it isn't generally as pretty in real life. People sometimes say the wrong things out of discomfort, confusion, or cattiness. We also misinterpret others' comments because of our own issues and insecurities. We're human, after all. This is why a lot of us end up disappointed when our lives don't tie up neatly with a bow after catharsis. Life isn't like the movies—at least my life, anyway.

For years, I told my friends that I wanted to write a book called *Kitchen Island Slop* because it would more accurately reflect the shitshow of my life. I thought others might also connect to that image: all messy and complicated—healing, but also real. I'd call the stories *badass* because of the truth and authenticity, but also because of the theme of survival.

I'd always have a deep laugh after announcing my idea.

I first voiced my desire to write such a book about fifteen years ago, but I still didn't do anything. It was easier to talk about a dream than to actually do something about it.

You see, while I've longed to write a book like *Kitchen Table Wisdom*, I kept comparing myself to Dr. Remen, and I always came up way short. I'm no guru. I'm no famous motivational speaker. I prefer sad movies to happy ones because I'm drawn to the authenticity of sadness and pain. I felt like too many people wouldn't want to hear the stories I'd pick.

Unfortunately, most of what I've learned in life has come from things ending badly. In fact, most of my personal growth has resulted from catastrophic error. The path has sometimes been ugly. My stories would be more reflective of this life experience: wild, crazy . . . sloppy. Even though I hoped there may be others who might connect to my shit-show, I wondered, would people read something like that?

I worried that people might pick up my book in search of *Chicken Soup for the Soul*² and end up with *Comfort Food* *for the Thighs*. For fifteen years, I concluded that I was not worthy of writing something people would want to read. Now I see that was a bullshit waste of time.

"Unworthy" is a label I slapped on myself because of fear. I had fear of being misunderstood. I had fear of not being good enough. I had fear of failure. I kept measuring myself against someone whom I could never be like and concluding that what I had to offer was not valuable, instead of seeing myself as equally valuable in different ways.

I began thinking of how many other people feel the same way. While some feel moved by inspirational story-telling, they may simultaneously feel as if their stories are too different or too messy. I can't tell you how many times I have heard people confess deep-seated fears in therapy, only to be surprised when I tell them they are far from being alone. Since people rarely talk out loud about their fears, everyone feels alone, isolated.

We certainly aren't seeing this kind of realness on social media—at least not on purpose.

And so, I decided to come out of the fear closet. I wrote this book for all the badasses who want to get real about life. These are the people who may feel or have felt not good enough and isolated by self-doubt and fear. I wrote this book for all the people who are ready to embrace the idea that we are all a little bit (or a lot) crazy and want to talk about it. And get this: these stories can also be inspirational!

Imagine for a moment a group of people hanging around the kitchen island, sharing and embracing the shitshow of life with safety, acceptance, and a deep sense of humor. It is not the laughing *at* but laughing *with* that provides a sense of connection and healing. This group recognizes that none of us are alone. We are more alike than we imagine. There is also a lot of cussing and confessing. Group members call out the bullshit with understanding and compassion. Everyone admits to personal "I've been there" moments. This realness is badass.

Over the last fifteen years, I've discovered that people like to hear messy stories too. It makes us feel *normal*, which increases our sense of connection.

I used to work in a medical office where I was famous for telling stories about my kids and parenting. It was a surefire way to get people to laugh, and I loved to create laughter at work. It made the day more fun.

One day, I was telling a colleague how I managed my latest parenting snafu. She laughed and said, "I love hearing your stories because they make me feel like a better parent!" This wasn't meant to be an insult. She went on to tell me she loved that we didn't have to pretend to be perfect; she meant that my stories helped others feel normal or typical—not less than.

Being out there with my wacky stories seems to break down a sense of shame or embarrassment when people feel like they don't measure up to the curated images on social media. My stories open the door to the flawed, awkward humans we really are, but with the knowledge that there are lots and lots of other people who are also there.

The false notion that inspiration and hope can come only from stories of neatness, beauty, and fairy-tale endings is a huge part of the problem. This isn't always life. In fact, it is rarely *real* life. Inspiration and hope are very often found in the everyday wrong turns, mistakes, and unexpected endings.

It's time to accept and embrace the shitshow of our lives. I have been afraid to publicly embrace my shitshow, and I'm guessing that you, too, worry about measuring up, being judged. We fret about being shunned. I'm not saying it is impossible to find acceptance. It is just hard—especially if we are too busy hiding our shitshows.

I have been a hypocrite because I tell people all the time to take risks and be vulnerable. Then, I saw Brené Brown's[3] Netflix special where she said she isn't interested in feedback from people who aren't also in the arena. I'd been telling lots of people to get into the arena, but I hadn't been willing to fully enter it myself.

That is why I include some of my own stories in this book. It's not because I view myself as badass, but I want to remind you that I am right there in the shitshow with you. I am no different, despite my professional degrees. We are in the trenches together.

When I use the term *shitshow*, it isn't because I am making fun of difficult and painful circumstances. Rather than a judgment, it is a nod to the fact that normal life is messy, and we benefit from managing our expectations with that messiness in mind. Shitshow means "the mess that is life." When we use the term *shitshow*, we claim ownership of our expectations, which is empowering.

This book is not about softness and finesse. It is not about grace and eloquence. These qualities are not my style, and I own that. If that is what you seek, this book isn't for you. This book is about the wild ride that is real life.

By now, you may have realized I have a hard time holding my tongue. I am known to argue negative self-talk with,

"That's bullshit! Fuck that." My methods are suspect in comparison to Dr. Remen's, although we share the same intention: to heal.

My messages can be rough and in your face. My style is to use saucy language to induce a smile and impart perspective. I want to share the lessons I've learned in life, but they are not always neatly packaged. My stories come from the times I have fucked up and made a mess. The stories in this book come from others who have also made very human mistakes.

Note of caution: Many of the stories do not include an element of humor. Some are gut-wrenchingly painful stories of abuse and end of life. They may be triggering, which is why I include some suggestions for finding a therapist at the end of the book. At the same time, these stories are inspirational and have an uplifting message. They are real, uncomfortable, and beautiful. I believe, though, that talking about life with this kind of authenticity enables healing.

After all these years, I feel this is what I am meant to do. I am meant to share foibles, missteps, and human nature with others who feel ashamed, embarrassed, and isolated. I am meant to bring it all into the light. Slop it out on the kitchen island. I am meant to be the real me—the true shitshow—because people need to hear that too.

Let me cut to the chase. Probably *the* most important life lesson is to be oneself. Though I may admire certain qualities in others, I may never have those qualities. That doesn't make the qualities I do have any less valuable. It also doesn't mean that I need to transform myself into something I can't be in order to pursue a dream.

This is what makes life so wonderful and colorful. We are all different, yet we all bring something to the table.

THE NITTY-GRITTY

MOMF

It is important to mention MOMF—which stands for Move on Motherfucker—because it will explain how I use profanity on purpose. Cursing isn't really a bad habit or sign of an unruly upbringing. Cursing is a scientifically supported stress management tool! MOMF is the methodical application of mindfulness, cognitive-behavioral therapy, humor, and profanity.[4]

I've written extensively about MOMF elsewhere, but here are some key points that will help you understand my general philosophy of healing. In short, MOMF involves:

- Understanding the genetic and life factors that create filters for the way we see the world, ourselves, and other people—especially if it is fucked up with "not good enough" filters. These filters are also called beliefs, and if they are messed up, it creates a foundation for a lot of pain and suffering. For example, if you believe you are not good enough, you'll never feel good enough. You will only see data that support this belief, and you'll ignore anything to the contrary.
- Recognizing the negative, judgmental things we say to ourselves based on our mistaken beliefs. This is called self-talk, and self-talk can be quite the judgmental bitch if left unchecked.

- Calling the negative self-talk out as an inner motherfucker who just needs to stop: stop judging; stop allowing bullshit; stop making choices that prolong the pain.

- Accepting that we are all motherfuckers. We are all crazy messes from time to time. We will make mistakes. We are human. It is okay. Let the judgment and self-abuse go.

- Developing profanity-laden counterstatements that we can use to call out our inner motherfuckers and laugh our asses off so that it hurts just a little less and enables us to move on.

This description is incredibly simplified. Just know that this book includes life lessons that have shaped and influenced my MOMF philosophy to recognize that we are all human motherfuckers and to embrace that with laughter in order to let go of the pain, guilt, and shame. I highlight some of the more impactful experiences I've had that have taught me something and hopefully will be instructive to you.

I want you to know, though, that although I do laugh at myself, I don't laugh at others. I don't make fun of people—but I do enjoy pointing out the funny, the ridiculous, the motherfucker things we all do. I feel it lessens the very real pain of feeling alone, the very real pain of feeling not good enough, the very real pain of feeling that we've done shitty things that can never be repaired.

Not everything in life is worthy of laughter. I deeply understand that and do not mean to suggest that we make fun of everything. I am merely saying that laughter can be an emotional release that allows us to detach from pain when necessary.

We've all been there. You are not alone. You are never

alone. The self-talk that tells you that you are alone, sub-standard, and not good enough is a fucking liar. The release of laughter around calling out the self-talk allows us to see it a bit more clearly.

While I am on the topic of explanations, some may object to my use of the word "crazy." I understand the objection. As a psychologist, I do not consider crazy to be a diagnosis, and I do not refer to people with a psychiatric disorder as "crazy." My approach to healing is to use everyday language that others use, and "crazy" is a common descriptor folks use to capture the essence of rollercoaster emotional reactions or internal chaos. My use of "crazy" is methodical based on how words are encoded with emotion in the brain. When we call out judgmental self-talk with words like "crazy," there is an emotional release. I do not consider it a derogatory word and object to the idea that people with psychiatric disorders associate themselves with that term. All of that said, I understand the reasoning behind the objection, but I hope you consider my intent, which can be overlooked in discourse. There are a variety of other controversial terms I use, but I've learned over the years that I cannot please everyone. I am simply going to be authentic myself (recall the most important life lesson above).

My anxiety monster, who has told me all of the ways people may misunderstand my approach, has been fed for the moment.

Journaling

Anyone familiar with my work knows that I recommend journaling liberally, but it isn't just a matter of preference. Going back to coursework in cognitive psychology, I remember learning about ways to improve memory. Lo and behold, notetaking is a key strategy. Think of journaling as a way to strengthen or deepen the lessons you want to learn.

Later in my fellowship training, I learned additional benefits of journaling. I discovered the work of Dr. James Pennebaker, who has thoroughly studied the health benefits of journaling. A multitude of studies demonstrate that journaling improves outcomes associated with diabetes, heart disease, insomnia, depression, anxiety, and post-traumatic stress disorder, to name a few.[5]

There are multiple theories as to why journaling works so well, including the overall benefits of outwardly confessing the things that weigh so heavily on our hearts. My hypothesis is that at any given point, we have too much on our minds. It can be chaotic. Taking time to put our thoughts and feelings into language creates meaning. Putting our experiences into words gives insight and creates understanding. Writing forces us to sort out the confusion in our heads, which can lead to healing. It also helps us ferret out the lessons we need to learn.

Journaling is a form of personal therapy, a session with oneself. It helps us see healthy and unhealthy themes in our thinking. I also believe that writing our feelings and experiences is a type of exposure therapy. Exposure therapy is when we expose ourselves over and over to thoughts, feelings, and experiences that we fear so that we become less afraid. Journaling allows us to sit with, understand, validate, and tolerate our feelings.

For all of these reasons, I include journaling prompts throughout the book. Let me be completely clear that the journaling prompts are not simply window dressing. They are scientifically based techniques that will help you reinforce your grit, improve your growth, nurture your hope, and allow your healing. They will not work unless you do them. No pain, no gain. I recommend that you give it value by choosing a dedicated notebook or fancy journal to track your progress.

Layout

This book is divided into teachable moment life themes: Grit, Growth, Hope, and Healing. These topics fit with so much of what I see in my personal and professional life. There is no way to cover everything. My goal is to hit the highlights. You will also note that the stories could fit into multiple themes. That is life. Nothing is neat, and that is why it is beautiful!

Special Note

The details of the stories within this book have been altered to protect the true identities of the persons involved. There are many times that I combine multiple similar stories into one narrative in order to emphasize a theme. Be assured that this method has allowed me to remain faithful to the spirit of the experiences while also staying true to what others share with me and respecting their trust.

No one should read a story in this book and know it is about them unless I sought out consent, which I did for a few stories. Any familiarity you feel with these stories is coincidental and proves my point that we have shared human experiences.

At the same time, I am prone to high anxiety, and my worry is that some who know me will read this book and feel left out. They may wonder: *was my story not badass enough?* Please know that every single person who has stepped foot into my office is badass for facing fears, sharing stories, and being vulnerable. It is simply impossible to write every story, but also, I carry aspects of every interaction into the stories I tell. While you may not see your specific story, know that parts are there in how my thinking has been shaped over the years. Yes, you are badass even if your particular story is not included.

GRIT

G rit is a never-give-up mindset. It is a passion to achieve a goal, a persistent determination to achieve.

When I think of grit, I think of stubbornness or a refusal to believe that something cannot be done. It is, in fact, an unyielding belief that something can be done despite the circumstances.

According to Dr. Angela Duckworth,[6] grit is a better predictor of successful goal attainment than talent. If you have talent in a certain area, that's great, but it doesn't mean you'll stick with the goal. Grit is a strong drive toward a goal that doesn't let up no matter what. Grit pushes a person to set higher and more challenging goals and energizes them to work harder to achieve them.

Failures, mistakes, mishaps—people with grit see all of these as part of the plan. They are useful data that will help in goal attainment. Grit is about not losing hope. Grit is being relentless.

I have noticed over the years that grit can be so much larger than a specific goal. Grit can be a passionate pursuit of feeling better and improving life situations. Grit can be a persistent drive to recover from trauma, hurt, and addiction. There are many other iterations.

People with grit recover from tragedy more quickly. They don't stop until things are better. People who have grit accept that pain is part of life, and while pain is never enjoyable, they see tolerating some pain as a means to lasting change. This outlook makes it easier to see pain's purpose. It doesn't hurt less. It's just accepted as part of the process.

Living with grit is incredibly courageous. It stirs a boundless drive for a better life, but it also ignites the conviction to face whatever comes. It fuels a tenacity to challenge demons, traumas, and hurts. It inspires the strength to be different despite all the forces that work against being different. When we make mistakes, grit gives us the audacity to get up. Every. Single. Time.

What if we all had a relentless drive to be our best selves and live our best lives? What if we never let anything keep us down for long? What if we were constantly setting new goals for personal growth? What if we had the courage to confront the lies we've been told to keep us in a certain lane?

Yeah, I know. It's pie in the sky, but how about *successive approximation*? Successive approximation is inching toward a goal and rewarding ourselves along the way. It is about getting there over time. I think having grit is realizing we will never be *there* anyway.

Of course, having grit doesn't mean that people never break down. Humans are not machines. Even the grittiest folks have pity parties. They get discouraged. People with grit just don't *stay* at the pity party. They are ready to move on, motherfucker. They understand that they can't always wait for the emotions to dissipate. People with grit know they need to act, and they trust that the heart and mind will eventually catch up. Behavior comes first.

So where does grit come from?

Grit is likely genetic for some people, but that doesn't mean that those without the genetic gift can't develop grit. It just takes more work.

How can a person build grit? This is the million-dollar question that educators, in particular, are working hard to understand so that they can teach it in school. Grit is about learning how to be good coaches to ourselves. Think about this for a moment. The best coaches encourage our virtues and help us compensate for our more challenging qualities or habits. They push us to stretch beyond familiarity and paralysis to the zone of productivity. Really great coaches help us develop the capacity to confront ourselves with brutal honesty, call out the bullshit when needed, give self-comfort where appropriate, and push like hell every step of the way. When you coach yourself to develop grit, you add arrows (and other weapons) to your quiver so you can fight the inner bullies that instill self-doubt. It is mustering the courage to stare down our fears even if we don't know what will happen next.

The key to developing grit is intentional self-reflection— deliberately studying ourselves for the purpose of understanding. It is about noticing what we do, how we do it, and why we do it. As we observe, we begin to connect how life experiences have shaped us and how we treat ourselves. In order for this to happen, we must dispense with cruel self-judgment, as we would with a best friend, and intentionally choose what to do with all the data.

Finally, one of the hardest components of grit is noticing your emotions and putting them aside—or what we call *detaching*—for a period of time because emotions aren't always productive. Grit is having the wherewithal to see emotions as booby traps in the path of life and choosing to step around them, while noting that they remain. It isn't about ignoring or denying emotions. What I am talking about is avoiding the pitfalls so that you can get the work done.

Take fear, for example. Fear may arise as we face challenges; that's natural and healthy. But if we fall prey to the fear, we will retreat. The retreat is the problem. Grit is the ability to notice the fear, detach from it, and push beyond it when necessary. In my view, this may be the hardest part of developing grit.

In the following pages I will share with you some stories of grit that inspire me. I hope you are able to find your own examples along the way.

After each story, I provide journaling prompts, and the end of each section offers even more reflective writing exercises. Below are some ideas to get you started.

JOURNAL PROMPTS

- Take some time now to deeply reflect on grit in your own life. How would you rate yourself on grit as a general quality of your personality?
- Describe some times you have shown grit.
- Describe some times when you have not shown grit.
- What intrigues you about grit as you think about your life?
- What will be your biggest obstacle to grit?
- What will be your biggest facilitator of grit?
- Why do you want to have more grit in your life?

Harnessing Grit

• • •

Amir was a scrappy go-getter. He told me straight up that he had one goal in life, and that was to be different from his family of origin. His father left the family when Amir was very young, and Amir had no relationship with him. Amir's mother abused alcohol and had a hard time holding a steady job. Amir felt forced into being "the man of the family" early on because no one else was there to take care of his younger brother.

Amir's first job was a paper route when he was twelve years old. He graduated to mowing lawns and shoveling snow. He was chief encourager to his brother and tried to ensure a sense of predictability around the house. Amir was an okay student, but he didn't enjoy school much. He had no one at home to encourage him to get good grades, and so, naturally, he let that part slide. After graduating from high school, Amir joined the police force because he thought it would be an exciting job, and he liked to help others.

All along, Amir continued to provide financial support to his mother and brother as much as he was able.

Time passed, and Amir got married and had a daughter of his own. He enjoyed a stable home life and kept in his mind's eye the image of the man, husband, and father he wanted to be rather than what he'd known. Life wasn't easy for Amir, but he knew how much harder it could be. He was grateful for the small things.

Just before Amir's daughter turned two years old, she was diagnosed with cystic fibrosis. Amir was heartbroken. At the same time, he felt even more driven to be the best dad he could be. He verbalized that his daughter was going to have the most normal life possible. What would have broken many people seemed to energize Amir to work even harder.

Then, one average day, while Amir was on duty, he was a first responder to the scene of a domestic violence hostage situation. Without fully thinking through the consequences, Amir jumped into rescue mode and sustained a bullet wound and a concussion. He was hospitalized for ten days and discharged home for continued outpatient therapy.

Amir had a mixture of emotions. He was proud that he saved others from harm's way, but he was frustrated that he was now unable to do his duties at work and home. He was also angry that his actions resulted in significant medical costs and disability. Because Amir had so many responsibilities to tend to, he expected to blow through rehabilitation like a champion. He was, after all, a force of nature.

If only it were that easy.

As the weeks dragged on, Amir was more irritable at home and in his therapies. He was having nightmares about the event. He started arguing with his wife, and he found himself withdrawing from his daughter. Amir was angry with himself for getting injured. He was angry that he wasn't healing faster. He was angry at the perpetrator of the violence. He was sick of sitting at home when there was so much he could be doing.

Amir was referred to me, and I diagnosed him with post-traumatic stress disorder (PTSD). Acute PTSD can present differently in different people, but for Amir, it was anger, irritability, avoidance of talking about emotions, difficulty concentrating, restlessness, and fear that bad things were going to happen—even though he didn't know what they were. He felt guilt and a sense of being outside of his own body watching himself walk through life (what we call *depersonalization*). He had sleep problems and nightmares.

At another time in his life, Amir would have been resistant to seeing a therapist, but by the time he was referred to me, he was desperate to feel better. He was willing to try anything—except medication. He didn't want to take any antidepressants or anxiety pills. He had weaned himself off pain medications a long time ago for fear of getting hooked.

Amir still possessed the spirit to power through, but he was lost.

I explained to Amir that treatment of PTSD is complex and takes a lot of courage. He would need to commit to channeling his energy into recovery, and Amir loved every word because all he heard was that there was something he could do to feel better. Amir had grit for recovery. Knowing *what* to do was the piece he'd been missing.

Amir recounted all the events surrounding the hostage situation. I asked him to write the entire story of the shooting and his subsequent recovery. I then asked him to add in connections to his early life experiences in order to develop a deeper understanding of what happened and how it all fit in with the person he is more broadly.

Where he had previously told himself to move on, Amir now allowed his feelings of guilt, anger, frustration, and sadness to flow. Before, he didn't know what to do with his feelings, so he denied them; however, they were still there. Amir was surprised to discover that expressing the feelings and naming them was actually doing something to feel better.

Counseling wasn't just a lot of feel-good mumbo jumbo.

Amir was able to associate his feelings about the shooting and sense of helplessness to unresolved feelings about a lost childhood and trauma due to things he'd witnessed as a child. As is often the case, traumas build upon themselves, which means that each new trauma connects to the previous. They fuel one another.

Amir confronted his drive to be a savior in his job as a first responder as a factor in the current incident, just as he'd tried to be the savior for his brother when he was a child. Amir was able to have compassion for himself, and eventually he was able to forgive himself for decisions that led to his injury and for all the perceived failures he'd been punishing himself for since childhood.

Every painful step of the process was challenging, and Amir showed up despite the pain, despite the fear that he might (and often did) uncover new sources of pain, and despite the fear that he might lose his mind along the way. Amir came to therapy, and it took a while.

Now, I would love to wrap this story up in a bow and tell you the fairy-tale ending, but that is not how life works. If my stories were straightforward and neat, they would only contribute to all the confusing and sometimes fake messages the world gives us, insisting that happy endings are required and that once we conquer an issue, it is in the past.

Life continued to throw curveballs to Amir. Life will always throw curveballs. Life is not a straight line. Life is not happily ever after. That is not the right message. Life is about getting up every day and facing what lies ahead to the best of our abilities. Some days will be great. Some days will be horrible. What is consistent is that each will pass. Having grit is the ability to move through and move past what is happening even when we don't want to face it.

Grit is about owning what we bring to the table, making the best of the good qualities, and minimizing the not-so-good qualities.

Amir returned to work as a police officer, and he began to rise in the ranks. Part of his process was maturing. He had to acknowledge that he could not save the world and that when he acted on that drive, he endangered himself and others around him.

Grit is seeing, acknowledging, accepting, and making it work. It is seeing what went awry and working hard to harness the energy for the good. Amir had the very commendable quality of wanting to help others, but his drive to do so could be reckless. In his case, grit needed harnessing. Sometimes our greatest strengths can also be our greatest vulnerabilities.

JOURNAL PROMPT

- I am sure this story about grit is surprising because it isn't a clear-cut success story but rather, a story of learning and understanding. Let's focus on you now. What strengths do you have that have also been your downfall at times? How have you learned to manage this tension?

Break the Cycle

. . .

One of the most disturbing problems I encounter in my practice is when people are haunted by bad childhoods. No matter how many times people go over and over the way a parent treated them, it never seems to make sense. Therefore, the pain doesn't go away. Because I see the lifelong aftermath, I recognize that I am often filled with rage at people who inflict so much harm on innocent, undefended children.

Frequently, the villainous person is the mother, and I think this exacts even more pain because of the image of all a mother should be. A mother *should be* nurturing, ever-loving, forgiving, and life-giving. We tend to give dads a pass when they let us down or even fail miserably at being a good father, but somehow, we just can't get past a mother who isn't loving or—even worse—is abusive. For a mother to be unattached or even abusive is so antithetical to our concept of mothering, our minds just can't make sense of it.

Since the archetype of a mother is one who gives all of herself for her child, it becomes incredibly hard to understand when this is not the lived experience. When this happens, I see grown adults become preoccupied with the idea that perhaps they were unlovable as a child. This creates another layer of abuse and trauma. There was the original insult, and then there is the secondary trauma of the adult once again judging and beating up the inner child.

Tina wasn't physically abused by her mother, but she was absolutely emotionally abused. She was the older of two children. Her father worked a lot and wasn't around. Tina's mother was a stay-at-home mom, and she had a lot of health concerns. In Tina's words, "Mom was always sick." Looking back, Tina believes that her mom gave birth to her in order to have someone to help out around the home. For as long as Tina can remember, she was cooking, cleaning, and waiting on her mother. In fact, as a child, Tina was told over and over that the reason her mother gave birth to her was so that she could take care of her mother.

Tina's mom was dependent on opiates and didn't like to leave the house much. This gave her mom a convenient excuse to not attend any of Tina's school functions. Tina learned to make excuses for her mother. She didn't have friends because her mother didn't want other kids hanging around the house. It was too stressful. Tina was also too busy taking care of her mother and her younger brother to go to other children's homes. She became an adult long before any child should have to do so.

Tina also remembers her mom as competing for attention at home. If Tina had a cold, her mom had a bout of migraines. If Tina had a stomach virus, her mom got the flu. If Tina's dad praised her for good grades, her mom would ask for compliments on her appearance. Tina can't remember one time that her mom was selfless. She can't remember her mother taking care of her. Her mom always seemed to be taking, although Tina never recognized that as a child.

Then there was the emotional abuse. Tina said that her mom complained aloud that Tina was a whiny taker. Her mom belittled her as needy if she asked for anything. She told Tina to toughen up when she called from school that she was sick. She told Tina that her father worked so much to get away from Tina's bad behavior. All the while, Tina was a straight-A student who never seemed to get into trouble. Tina's brother sometimes called Tina "mama" because Tina was so involved in taking care of him.

When I met Tina as an adult, she was incredibly pleasant. She had learned to put on a happy face because that's what people wanted to see. Tina sought counseling because she was unhappy in life, but she insisted that she had nothing to be unhappy about. She told me that there must be something wrong with her that she couldn't be happy.

Tina was still a primary caregiver to her mother, who remained ever critical and ungrateful. Her father had died five years earlier. Her brother had moved far away. Tina had been married for five years, but she had no children. She was afraid that she would not be a good mother, so she'd avoided it. Her husband was an incredibly nice guy, who was quiet and kept to himself. Tina felt alone in the home and in her marriage. She enjoyed her professional career, but her coworkers dumped on her excessively. Tina could not fathom saying no. She never felt good enough, and she self-criticized her every move.

After many months of therapy, Tina came to recognize just how deeply her mother had failed her and how the intense, enduring emotional abuse of childhood deeply impacted her sense of self. Tina could see it. She understood how she had taken over the role of her mother in now beating herself up. She could identify how her negative self-talk impacted her function, and she was deeply sad about it all. Despite understanding what had happened in her childhood and the relationship of those experiences to her present unhappiness, Tina could not get past ruminating on the question, *why did my mother do this to me?*

Questions of *why* haunt me. I can provide an intellectual answer of *how* people like Tina's mother fail. I can describe *what* they do and the consequences. I can even explain the underlying personality defects that cause such failings. Yet I can never adequately get at the *why* someone would not love or show love to a child. Such questions are beyond understanding.

What is worse is that a person with a normally functioning attachment and sense of self cannot comprehend an inability to love and show love for a child. No amount of time spent contemplating provides a satisfactory answer. When it's your own mother who seems to have chosen not to love, it cuts to the core. I try to explain that there is likely an inability to love, but that still is hard to digest.

People get stuck in *why* and cannot move on because they believe the why will provide some clue about themselves. They have been so brainwashed into believing that they are unlovable and not good enough that they want to look deeply within to see what is wrong with them to justify why a parent would be so terrible. When they can't find it, they just keep digging deeper. Unfortunately, the answers aren't there.

The only insight I can share is that some people are incredibly and irreparably damaged for a variety of reasons. They are not capable of unconditional and selfless love, yet they still have children. It isn't that there is something wrong with the child. There is something wrong with the adult. Unfortunately, intellectually understanding that does not somehow magically make it go away. The hurt, the pain, and the memories are still there. No matter how you look at them, it will never make emotional sense such that it hurts less. All one can do with any of it is to work hard to detach from it.

Sorting through all of this means emotionally digesting what happened. It is reflecting with new eyes—those of an adult. It is sorting out what was the parent's, what was the child's, and what is your own. It is recognizing that as an adult, you are now capable of giving love to the inner child who still seeks comfort and nurturance. It is stopping the cycle of abuse.

The tragedy of what happened in childhood is real, but it cannot be rewritten. The suffering that comes from self-blame and trying too hard to understand why a flawed person is flawed and behaves in flawed ways—well, that suffering is self-induced. That self-induced suffering is under our control. It isn't easy, but we can stop this suffering at any time.

Here is where it gets really frustrating. People are desperate to feel better, and they ask how. All you can do is notice what you are feeling. Notice that you are starting to analyze and overthink. Then, do whatever works to redirect your attention. Call a friend. Journal. Exercise. Take a walk. Read. Do a visualization exercise. Once you put a plan into practice and do it over and over again, it will get easier. Unfortunately, there is no quick fix. There is only self-care, one day at a time.

The point is to stop the cycle of abuse. That part is under our control.

Tina was overwhelmed with everything that she faced. She chose to start by allowing herself to feel. While this may sound strange, it was huge. Tina had been told so often over the years that her feelings didn't matter. She had not allowed herself to feel anything that might be negative or might bring others around her down. Tina started with allowing herself to not smile or be friendly when she didn't feel like it. She progressed from that to allowing herself to say no. She allowed bad moods. She practiced acknowledging that her feelings were valid and acceptable.

We talked about how Tina was now responsible for being a good parent to herself and not continuing the cycle of abuse. Tina benefited from allowing herself the freedom to be as she is. She started having more deeply genuine conversations with others, sharing her true feelings rather than just saying what she believed others wanted to hear.

Tina allowed herself self-care. She began to exercise and journal. She started reading for fun. She began to really see her true self and not the veneer she'd created for maximum acceptance.

At the end of this arm of our work, Tina was working on forgiveness. She was writing unsent letters to her mother and her father. She was writing a letter to herself. All of this involved a complete inventory of the things that she felt caused hurt in her life. We felt it was important to name what happened and acknowledge it as valid. Once she'd acknowledged her experience, Tina needed to write about it and make a commitment to moving forward. She knew this process would take time, but she was ready. She was also working to identify the legacy of self-abuse and stop it by arguing back with herself.

The challenges will be lifelong for Tina as for so many of us, but Tina had the grit to unpack it all, especially when it felt excruciating, which was most of the time. It took grit to tolerate the pain that could not be fully understood. It took grit to do the work anyway. Tina practiced self-care and self-acceptance even when she didn't feel she deserved it. She learned that the feelings of self-denial were mistaken. Tina also learned that the time she spent healing was working—just not on the timeline she wanted, which was immediately.

In Tina's case, grit was having the strength and courage to face down the demons that cut to the core, which include foundational relationships with people who are supposed to love us and treat us with love. Grit is being able to tolerate never having an explanation that will make sense; grit is having the faith that you are doing the right thing; and grit is accepting that the story will be okay in the end.

JOURNAL PROMPT

- What is your go-to style of managing uncertainty and questions of "why" that have no adequate answers? What unresolved conflicts does this story bring up for you? Make some notes so you can come back to it.

The Lens Makes All the Difference

. . .

For some people, grit is a positive mindset on steroids. I enjoy positivity, but I also understand that positivity can be judgmental. Positivity can be misused by telling oneself to just think happy thoughts. When overused, positivity can be a way of telling yourself that feeling bad in a bad situation is wrong. While there is a place for positivity, grit requires a balanced approach.

Part of grit is continually attacking barriers until you overcome them. It is about being brutal at times about what isn't getting done. But unchecked grit can lead to a hyper-focus on errors or what isn't working. To be ultimately successful with grit, you'll need to also create time to acknowledge what is working well—what *is* getting done.

The approach of *only* focusing on things to be improved and problems to solve doesn't work. How can we expect to know what we are doing right if we focus only on what we are doing wrong?

I coach executives on wellness and, by and large, they are wildly successful in their career trajectories. They have successfully managed most challenges and are superbly calm problem solvers. They are also fantastic about encouraging talent on their teams. Managing people is what they do well.

Another thing I have found to be commonplace among executives is that they are great at anticipating problems in order to stay ahead. They are *keenly aware* of the problems. It is human nature to be on alert for the next problem around the corner. It is what keeps us alive. But it is also what keeps us beaten down.

Marcel was a senior supply chain director within a large organization. He was accustomed to long hours, wildly fluctuating expectations, and multiple barriers associated with international trade. Marcel liked his job, but he admitted it was probably taking years off his life. When COVID-19 hit, it was like a bomb dropped into his world. Marcel quickly became physically and emotionally exhausted with the multitude of problems that he could not control. We spent multiple visits where I cajoled him to adjust expectations and practice mindfulness in order to cope with all of the colliding expectations and family and health worries.

As Marcel felt his work world was spinning wildly out of control, I asked him to take time each day to write down at least one thing he accomplished or could be proud of. I shared with Marcel that, even in everyday life, we can become so consumed with the next problem or set of problems that it is easy to lose sight of what we actually achieved.

When people take time and summarize the achievements at the end of the year, they are generally surprised and even moved by the sheer magnitude of what they got done. The problem is that we lose sight of everything that happens during the year. This is why writing down accomplishments daily can be a valuable tool for not losing sight of the progress that may be measured in inches rather than miles.

Think of how a coach teaches a student a new skill. Progress is measured in approximations, and to be effective, a coach cannot just give negative feedback or no feedback at all until the student masters the skill. That would be counterproductive. Effective coaching is giving micro feedback all along the way, including reinforcing and encouraging what is going well. So why don't we do that with ourselves? We somehow just don't take the time, and the negatives and problems and burdens consume our attention. Forcing ourselves to consider and acknowledge the positives is a skill and practice that will make it more likely to be successful in the future.

When Marcel did this practice daily, he was surprised at how much he was getting done. He enjoyed the feeling associated with documenting progress. In fact, he noted that writing down the accomplishments increased his overall awareness of small things he was missing. He became more appreciative of the many interactions where he was able to be a positive influence in his team members' lives. Surprisingly, he found many meaningful moments with others that he'd simply overlooked because they weren't centered on a *problem*, which was all he was previously able to see. Marcel learned to recognize that he'd been measuring his efforts with the wrong tool, and that made all the difference in the world.

Grit is reminding yourself to look around at the whole picture for what you may be missing. It's about building on the positives and not being afraid to take a moment to say to yourself, "Nice job!" When you have grit, you are always looking at what can be improved, but always looking at what is wrong or missing can turn into a cancer of the mind. A singular focus like this can be demoralizing. True grit is forcing yourself to also look at what has gone well—what you've achieved—and then visualizing how each success takes you one step closer to where you want to be. If you don't take time to notice the steps, it is too easy to find yourself lost on the journey.

JOURNAL PROMPT

- What is your go-to self-coaching style? How would you rate yourself on your ability to see what you're getting done within the shitshow of life? How can you better remind yourself of accomplishments even when they are hard to see? (Hint: How do you help others with recognition?)

Show Up for the Fight

. . .

Textbooks and statistics have taught me that childhood abuse often has devastating consequences for adult survivors. But reading these facts did not prepare me well for hearing real-life experiences. Abusive experiences are scars of the heart that continue to haunt people, and I have learned that no matter what I say, sometimes they never fully heal.

Occasionally, though, I meet people like Leighlah. Leighlah first consulted me as an eighteen-year-old who was heading off to college. She had paralyzing anxiety, which presented as a fear of vomiting in public. Leighlah did have a couple of episodes of vomiting in social situations, and she worried it would happen again. Now she wasn't sure she could make it to college, which was to start in a few months.

I'd seen fear of vomiting before, and I knew exposure therapy was highly efficacious. I assigned Leighlah reading and exposure exercises, and she nailed them. Our therapy quickly morphed into tackling romantic relationship issues, and it was clear that Leighlah had a high need to control herself, the environment, and others. A high need to control is common among those with anxiety, so that was not surprising.

The lie people with anxiety tell themselves is that if they work hard enough, they can control people and things around them. This is a misguided attempt to reduce anxiety by predicting what will happen next. Predicting what will happen next comes from controlling what will happen next. However, this doesn't work long-term because control is an illusion.

Leighlah and I discussed the need for control and how to manage it. I understood that it would be a long-term struggle, and Leighlah was up to the task. She owned it.

Leighlah came back to see me off and on. She broke up with her boyfriend because she realized that she couldn't control him, and when she saw the person he actually was, he wasn't attractive to her any longer.

Despite Leighlah's growing recognition that the drive to control wasn't helpful in human relationships, she used it to absolutely excel in college. As I've mentioned before, sometimes our greatest strengths are also our greatest challenges, and in this case our challenges can be strengths in other contexts.

During our visits, Leighlah had opened up about her home life. She felt constantly criticized by both of her parents in different ways. Her mom almost always minimized her concerns and completely ignored her achievements. Leighlah struggled to understand whether she was indeed a whiny brat or if her mom was too hard on her. Similarly, her dad critiqued her appearance constantly, as if he were her professional manager. Leighlah admitted that being at college, away from an environment she came to view as toxic, was good for her.

Leighlah applied and was admitted to medical school. She was elated. Her family seemed more concerned about how her being so busy would negatively impact the family, but they grudgingly congratulated her. While Leighlah was disappointed that they didn't come to visit her in medical school, which was only a few hours away, she came to realize that their absence was actually a blessing.

Leighlah continued intermittent counseling. She would come in and learn some new things about herself and depart and work on those things in real life. When she got stuck, she would come back. She had a string of unhealthy and, at times, emotionally abusive relationships. She struggled to understand why she behaved in ways that undercut her worth. She allowed shady men into her life knowing they were shady, and she allowed them to treat her in demeaning ways. Leighlah owned that she played an active role in enabling those interactions. She voiced commitment to overcoming the pattern.

Meanwhile, Leighlah rocked medical school. She was at the top of her class, won research awards, and found herself developing a strong sense of professional accomplishment despite the fact that her family demonstrated little interest or support.

One day, she was voicing frustration about the parallels between her trying to win over shady men and her trying to win over her family. Suddenly she spilled out that her uncle had molested her repeatedly as a young child. Based on her memory, she believed her parents knew about it and had brushed it aside.

Leighlah's parents were very into outward appearances, especially physical ones, and Leighlah connected how she'd been groomed to value her physical appearance above all else and use that to garner attention from men. Leighlah was filled with disgust. She voiced hatred for what her parents had done to her and hatred for how she'd behaved as a result.

Leighlah and I spent hours processing all of this over the course of multiple visits, and she voiced a commitment to change, yet she didn't entirely know what this meant. She graduated medical school and started her own practice. Though she continued to struggle with boundaries around her family as she recognized their toxicity, she didn't want to cut off contact.

Leighlah got married and had children. She continued to seek consultation around triggers and family-related concerns. She actively sought to be a different mother than the one she was born with. She recognized that life would continue to present her with challenges that she may or may not understand. What she could control was having an open mind and heart. What she could do was reflect. What she could focus on was showing up for the fight and giving her best.

When I think of grit, I think of people like Leighlah. She showed up to fight inner demons over and over and over in different scenarios even though the pain was excruciating. Leighlah committed to going deeper and pushing harder. Her journey led to her confronting the fact that people who she thought loved her didn't love her in a healthy way. She had to verbalize that and internalize the long-term impact in order to decide what to do with it.

When Leighlah thought back, she connected her vomiting to an outward sign of how sick she felt inside. Her environment made her sick. She denied it, and her body reacted with vomiting. Back then, she wasn't ready to name the actual problem, yet with grit, we finally got there.

Leighlah eventually distanced herself from her family of origin in order to limit their influence on her, but she chose to keep them in her life. Leighlah also built a completely separate and loving family comprised of friends who gave her all the acceptance her family of origin could not.

Some people may say, "What choice did Leighlah have?" We always have a choice. Leighlah could have continued to participate with her family of origin in ways that were abusive. She could have given in to feelings of defeat. She could have perpetuated the abuse she learned from her family in other relationships—choosing to surround herself with others who were abusive. She could have perpetuated the abuse with her own children.

No. Instead, Leighlah chose to fight for every inch of empowerment to be different. She has grit on steroids because she understands that the fight will never end. She knows that she can never let down her guard, and she has the courage to sit with that and own it.

JOURNAL PROMPT

- What demons have you faced down or do you need to face down? Where do you get the courage to keep going when it feels overwhelmingly hard?

Know Your Worth

. . .

Right out of graduate school, I completed a two-year fellowship in health psychology and medical education. I also got married to a man who had a well-established career. Because the work I wanted was highly specialized within graduate medical education, there were few jobs available where we lived. I went a full year piecing together gigs here and there until a more stable job came around. I didn't feel well-positioned to negotiate for what I really wanted. In other words, I was desperate.

This was a mindset mistake, and it is a mistake I see women make all of the time. Women, more so than men, feel compelled to compromise what we want in jobs. We willingly accept explanations that reimbursement could not possibly go higher due to budgetary constraints. We undercut our worth by asking for low-ball salaries. We tell ourselves that it's okay because we have to be team players; we will need more flexibility for children and family activities; and we don't want to be seen as a bitch.

And . . . there it is.

I believe women have an unspoken and pathological fear of being called or perceived as a bitch, and that fear drives women to behaviors that undercut their own value. While some of these behaviors may be genetic among women, I believe socialization—overt and covert—plays a strong role. Women see their mothers model self-sacrifice. They see their mothers behave in overly giving and deferential ways. Women see their mothers do whatever needs to be done in order to make the special sauce at home work.

Women also receive messages from a very young age about what it is like to be a well-behaved young *lady*. A well-behaved young lady doesn't ruffle feathers. Women *should be* liked. They *should be* pleasing. They *should really be* whatever they need to be in order to make it work. To be a bitch is to be *other* and not a part of the group.

I've heard the evolutionary idea that women are more compromising because they need to get along in groups, while men are bolder and more self-centered to hunt and protect. Regardless, it is time for all of that bullshit to die.

I've met with countless women of all ages who are contemplating new jobs. They have all expressed some level of appreciation for the opportunity in front of them. They have all expressed excitement for the promise of what was ahead. The problem is that, almost without exception, they approach these situations with ideas of what they want but are ready to open the discussion with low-ball expectations.

Samantha was an experienced communications director who was ready for new horizons. She worked her ass off, and her current job was a one-way road to nowhere. She'd interviewed for a new job and was told to expect an offer.

She told me what she dreamed of, what she feared, and what her next move was.

I asked Samantha to stop and consider what she was bringing to the table. She paused, clearly wondering what in the world I meant. She was just Samantha, in a shitty job, with an exciting new opportunity. She was grateful. Why was I being a downer?

I reminded Samantha that she brought maturity, work ethic, creativity, and leadership to the table. I reminded her of the situations she'd described to me where she may have been the only mature, decisive adult present. I reminded her of the times when all the shit rolled downhill to her desk, and she made a shit sandwich, which she then ate. I reminded Samantha of where she had taken her department with her leadership. I reminded Samantha that she had credentials and high intrinsic value.

I advised her that it was not okay to undersell. I asked what she believed her skills were worth. I asked why she wasn't putting the whole package out there at the front end of the conversation.

Samantha gave the expected responses. *The economy isn't good.* (Amazingly, the economy never seems to be good when women are being offered jobs.) *This is a great opportunity. I don't want to screw it up.* Then, of course, *I don't want to come off as a bitch.*

You see, men don't think that way. And it isn't that I am suggesting that women should be like men in order to be better. Women cannot, however, expect to be treated better and compensated commensurate with men if we don't demand our worth. It sets the expectation that we are willing and happy to accept less than.

What I am saying is that women will never be on the same playing field as men if we don't walk onto that field with confidence (even if we're only going through the motions until our hearts catch up).

When I was in a particular health-care organization, I recruited a male colleague for a new role. As the position emissary, I was asked to inquire as to his salary requirements. He told me what he thought was fair, and I thought to myself, *Wow. I bet they won't give you that much because they're tight, but good for you for asking.*

Because I had never been privy to this kind of negotiation before, I expected leadership to try and negotiate down. I'd never seen the kind of money this guy was asking for, and I had similar experience and credentials.

The leadership team did not blink. They made it happen. One of the senior female executives pulled me aside and said, "Are you okay that this person will be making more money than you?" I replied honestly, "Thank you for asking. It is truly okay as his responsibilities are quite different." I meant it; the position he wanted was a lot more work than I was interested in doing—but the whole experience opened my eyes. I did find it very interesting that it took a woman executive to even wonder how I might feel in comparison.

I was able to see from a different perspective how most men don't think twice about asking what they feel they are worth. There is no guilt. There is no second-guessing. They just put it out there, and no one else second-guesses it either. There was absolutely nothing wrong with the way this all went down.

I saw the same thing when my husband was later negotiating a position. Men aren't embarrassed or coy. They give a self-assured number, and the hiring entity feels comfortable that they are getting their money's worth. The self-confidence is actually attractive to the hiring party.

After Samantha and I had a real conversation about all of this, she admitted that once she was sitting around with some colleagues who were sharing salary information. The lone guy in the group reported making more money than any of the women, even though he was not the most senior of the group. They were all shocked and he shared how the hiring conversation had gone. He had simply asked for more upon hire, while the women had accepted the first offer.

Grit is about knowing what you bring to the table without feeling guilty about it. It is about valuing all that you have to offer and not feeling shame in asking for fair market value.

Grit is about not short-selling yourself and your value, and if you make an exception, it needs to be strategic. I've told women who insist on accepting a lower salary than they feel they are worth to request an official review of salary and benefits at six months. The strategy is short-selling with the communicated expectation up front that it is not okay or permanent. Think of it as clearly communicating that everyone in the room should know that this is a bargain that will not be tolerated long-term.

I've also told women to insist on other types of compensation when the salary cannot possibly be raised to fair market value. Instead, an applicant can request extra time off in lieu of monetary compensation. It isn't a black-and-white issue. There are still levers to pull.

Another thing that women don't consider enough is the status to be gained in titles. If a woman takes a job with a lower salary than she feels she deserves, she can require a specific title that will lend credibility while she seeks a new job. Titles, in general, are stepping-stones.

Women need to think more strategically so that they send the message, *I'm watching. I will persist. I won't give up. This is my life.* While women may have been socialized to see this as being a bitch, it is not. That pejorative thinking is meant to keep women in their convenient place, and it needs to stop.

While this guidance has been focused on women, it isn't just for women. It applies to anyone who tends to under-sell themselves. Men have been socialized to ask for their worth more easily, but there are exceptions. The concerns are more pervasive among women, but we all need to stop giving away our talents to organizations that exploit that generosity because we allow them to do so.

Grit is facing up to the uncomfortable truth that organizations will seek to get a bargain even through exploiting gender inequities, but we have a personal responsibility in shaping the change we seek. Grit is owning the discomfort and finding the courage to be our own best support without feeling guilty about it.

JOURNAL PROMPTS

- Take a seriously objective look at yourself. Write down the qualities and experiences you bring to the table. What are these truly worth? How can you better represent your value in situations where you tend to settle?

• One surefire way to boost your confidence is to develop a portfolio. Get a binder and create tabs for your valuable qualities identified in your journal. Insert the evidence, which are examples of presentations, projects, evaluations, achievements. When you doubt your worth, you can review your portfolio. After you've done your portfolio, write more about how you feel about yourself now.

Play the Hand You Are Dealt

. . .

From the time Chaundra was born, the cards seemed stacked against her. Her mom was dependent on alcohol to function and had a string of boyfriends who used and sold drugs. The household was completely unstable. As a ten-year-old, Chaundra was the only functioning adult in the home.

Despite all this, she survived. She got her brother and herself to school. She made good grades. She sought out scholarships and aid packages, and she went to college. All the while, Chaundra was still the only mature adult in her family unit.

Chaundra persisted. She got her degree in marketing and got a job. On the side, she was cleaning up her mother's messes and trying to be a stable presence for her brother.

Chaundra got married to a really nice guy and had a couple of children. Then, her husband developed a debilitating illness, and one of her children died. Chaundra gave up sleep. She strategized. She worked to exhaustion. And then she crashed.

Chaundra was angry. She was devastated. She was paralyzed with anxiety. Chaundra had one hundred other emotions she couldn't even name. We had to unwind the entire story, and it was incredibly painful. There were absolutely times that Chaundra was at her wits' end because she didn't know what to do with all her emotions. She didn't want to sit with them. She didn't want to feel them. She didn't want to process them. She wanted to move beyond them, but what she knew to do was no longer working.

Even though meeting with me was a first-class ticket to Shitsville in terms of guaranteed sadness, Chaundra never missed a visit. She persevered. In fact, Chaundra was going to prove to me, to others, and to herself that she was tough enough to endure and conquer. And she did.

Every time we met, I told Chaundra to exercise, and she resisted. She had excuses. She was tired. Everyone needed her more than she needed exercise. She tried to avoid in-depth discussion of feelings because "there was not much point."

I asked Chaundra to read *Codependent No More*.[7] She rolled her eyes at the thought of more work, but she did it anyway.

Chaundra was in a state of paralytic conflict. She was afraid to let go into overwhelming emotions, but she wanted to prove to me and herself that she was strong enough to face them down.

Then it was as if someone turned the light on, and Chaundra woke up. It may be more accurate to say that Chaundra hit rock bottom and hit it hard. She had run out of gas and could no longer ignore that she was doing everything for everyone else, and there was nothing left for her. There would never be a *someday* until she made it, and others would never learn to do for themselves as long as she was there to do it for them. At the same time, Chaundra recognized that she had been brainwashed to be this way since she was born.

This epiphany literally changed the direction of Chaundra's life.

At that visit, Chaundra said she was going to start exercising. Chaundra went to the gym, and she never stopped going there. She said exercising made her feel alive and healthy. She could also control exercise, and it felt like the only thing in her life that was controllable.

Chaundra wanted to know more about health and the body, and she started studying health science. She obtained a degree in Sports, Fitness, and Nutrition and started a coaching business. Chaundra faced down her personal demons, and she kicked their asses.

When I asked Chaundra how she was able to be so successful given how little support she received in early life, she looked me in the eye and said, "I have no idea, but I just kept getting up each time I fell down. I never stopped getting up."

Chaundra understood grit, and while life wasn't fair to her, it would be too easy to flail in a victim mentality. In fact, she would be justified in feeling like a victim, but Chaundra understood that there was nothing to be gained there. In fact, she hated everything about feeling like a victim. She could also continue to live the familiar life of self-sacrifice because it was familiar, but Chaundra was willing to imagine something else—even if it was scary. By choosing to expect more from herself and by never settling for *good enough*, Chaundra created her own path. This was a path that required her to stop avoiding self-care with the excuse that she had no choice.

Her life hadn't been perfect and would never be perfect, but Chaundra was comforted that there will always be something to work on—to keep her interested and invested. In some respects, grit starts with owning your own choices. It is all about understanding what cards you have—both good and bad—and making conscious decisions about how to play that hand to the best of your ability. Mostly, grit is about having the guts to take the risk of entering the game.

JOURNAL PROMPT

- In tough situations from your past, how have you played the hand you were dealt? Consider if your tendency is to take the mindset of victim or survivor. What do you think the difference is?

The Long Game

...

I don't typically treat folks for primary substance-use disorders because I believe it is a specialized field for which I am not qualified. I am also not patient enough or skillfully able to tell if someone is blowing smoke my way. When Damon consulted me ten years ago, it wasn't for substance use, but it was so obvious even I couldn't miss it.

Damon had lingering anger about the death of his older sister when he was a teenager. She was partying with friends. The driver was intoxicated and hit a tree. Damon's sister was thrown from the vehicle and died instantly. We first met fifteen years after her death, but Damon described it as if it were yesterday. He described nightmares with images of her dying and lying in a casket. Damon described episodes of intense anger at the teenager who was driving the car. Damon loved his sister so much, and he felt like he just couldn't get over losing her.

Damon had a great job and strong social support, and he was in a committed relationship. He just felt like he'd been haunted by her death for too long and wanted to deal with it.

As I was taking a history, Damon was quite honest about his alcohol use. He drank at least six to eight beers a day. Hard-core alcohol was on Thursdays, Fridays, Saturdays, and Sundays, with beer and hard liquor combined. He admitted to frequent arguments with his partner about weekend use since every weekend he would black out and not remember his behavior the previous night. He would feel horrible the next morning before starting again. Damon reported that during the blackouts he would pick fights with his partner and act badly, but he was not sure why.

When I told Damon that he was drinking way too much and that this was a problem, he laughed. He was very social, and alcohol use was a central component of social gatherings. He stated that he could not possibly stop drinking because he would have no friends or social life.

I told Damon that there was no possibility of relieving his emotional distress, anxiety, and low mood if he continued drinking. I provided education on alcohol use. I offered support for getting sober, but Damon told me in no uncertain terms that he was not stopping.

This is typically when folks leave and never return, but Damon was different. He asked if there was anything else I could do.

I offered brief grief counseling, which kept Damon engaged. We also did some couples counseling focused on conflict management, but I continued to reiterate that no intervention would be successful if Damon continued to drink. It was also clear that Damon's partner was also a heavy drinker, and this was common to their connection. Damon's partner likewise was not interested in stopping alcohol use.

Damon eventually gave in a bit and told me that he wanted to cut back on alcohol use and was going to try that for a while.

I should pause to mention that while I don't do primary substance-use counseling, I do have a strong belief that most people, particularly those with a family history of substance abuse, should have a goal of complete abstinence from alcohol. I believe that certain people have a genetic predisposition to alcohol abuse and dependence. I am not a believer in learning to control use. Alcohol is, after all, a substance that impairs judgment and decision-making. So, I continued to advise Damon and his partner to stop drinking.

As Damon was trying to cut back, he called me one evening in tears, obviously intoxicated. He told me that he wanted to die and hung up on me. I had no idea where he was. I had no idea who he was with. I was shaken to the core because I didn't know what to do. I called Damon's partner and got him to look for Damon. In retrospect, I don't know if this was right or even enough, but it was the choice I made.

Damon was at the cemetery. His partner took him home.

The next time I met with Damon, I told him that I would call the police if he ever did that again. He was embarrassed and acknowledged that trying to cut back on drinking wasn't working. He stated that he still wasn't ready to quit alcohol. He denied depression and stated that his grief was better. I told myself that at least I taught him some self-soothing skills other than alcohol use.

Damon came to see me off and on for the next eight years. Mostly, he had the same relationship concerns or he wanted to complain about feeling badly—emphatically stating that stopping drinking was off the table. At the same time, Damon would consistently ask questions about what getting sober would entail. He'd ask about his options and then go on with life.

One day I got a call from one of Damon's friends that he was checking into an inpatient recovery center and wanted me to know. He phoned me from time to time while inside the program to ask my opinion on treatment. When Damon got out, he was scheduled to see a substance abuse therapist. He called to tell me about how he hated the person and wanted a different referral, which I gave.

Damon fell off the wagon a few times. He did see another substance abuse therapist, who was helpful, but he stated that he wanted to see me again. I agreed to a few visits, and we talked about working the program and doing whatever he could to stop drinking. I *strongly* recommended journaling for all of the reasons I described in the introduction to this book. I *strongly* suggested finding a new social support system. I *strongly* reinforced the importance of regular exercise.

The biggest issue for Damon was coming to terms with his partner's continued alcohol abuse. Damon told his partner that if they were to remain together, the drinking would have to stop. His partner chose not to change, and Damon was crushed, although not surprised. Damon left the relationship, and we processed the pain associated with that.

Damon is now two years sober. He found a new social support system, a new committed relationship, and a new outlook on life. Damon told me that he never imagined that he could be so happy and so clear-headed. He never knew life could be so beautiful. The alcohol clouded all of that and led to guilt, anger, and distress.

It was a vicious cycle.

I think Damon and I both had grit in this situation. I wanted to give up on Damon because we had different goals, but I hung in there with the desperate belief that change was still possible. Damon did not have the goal of stopping alcohol use, but he had the goal of feeling better. He heard my opinion and wanted to try other things. He did, and they didn't work. He kept showing up, though, to push and to learn. Eventually, he went for it, and it paid off.

Damon was also testing me to see if I really believed. Even when Damon didn't believe in himself, he knew I believed. There was more than eight years of evidence.

The odds against alcohol abstinence are staggering. According to DrugAbuse.com,[8] rates of relapse range from 70 to 90 percent. In my opinion, anyone who tells me that they are actively fighting a substance-use disorder has grit. First of all, there is finding the strength to fight. Then there is committing to giving up the substance, making and working a plan, and sticking to the plan every day. Even harder, it seems, is getting back on the plan when things go off-script. It is a never-ending fight against genetics, biological cravings, emotional triggers, and habits that takes every ounce of effort.

Maybe the hardest part about getting sober is facing up to massive change on every level.

When Damon did diverge from his plan and drink again, thankfully he was drawn back to the peace and tranquility of being sober through years of learned skills. He was also compelled to avoid the drama, guilt, and physical pain associated with the poison of alcohol. Even more, Damon finally had a sense of peace around his sister's death. It was as if the alcohol that he had been using to numb the pain was actually enhancing it.

Damon taught me that behavior change doesn't always happen at the time help is offered, and this isn't failure. There isn't a schedule. However, when someone is curious and interested in learning more, behavior change is possible even years later, but the person has to be ready.

This is a story about persistence, pain, patience, and recovery. The path isn't straight and narrow. It is wide and winding. Every day is a new beginning if we allow it to be. It starts with showing up with an open mind to learn. What happens next is unwritten.

JOURNAL PROMPT

- Changing long-term patterns is incredibly challenging. Think of a time when you took on a really tough change in your life or helped someone else to change. What kept you going? What did you learn along the way?

The Grit of Risk

. . .

Humans are . . . well . . . human. Humans make bad decisions. Humans make mistakes. Humans fuck things up. Humans react based on emotions and fatigue. Humans misbehave in groups.

Test me on this—it seems that in any group there will always be a bad actor. This holds true for families, friend groups, and workgroups. It isn't even that the bad actor is a bad person. It is just one of those weird phenomena about group dynamics. Someone will generally act out. So, when I see it, I say to myself, *Oh, there it is. It had to happen that way. I don't need to judge it.* Somehow just knowing this and stepping back allows me to get less frustrated.

I don't expect perfection from humans. In fact, I expect people to show up for appointments telling me they fell back into old patterns, that they didn't follow through on what they said, and that they screwed up. Knowing that people are mistake-prone helps when I see people who have been unfaithful in committed relationships.

It isn't that I don't believe that couples can be faithful.

It isn't that I condone infidelity. It is just that I know that human beings are complicated. In other words, shit happens.

I have heard people say that they don't know how it happened. They just found themselves in unfaithful interactions. Their partners, who are on the receiving end of the infidelity, often view this explanation as a cop-out, and I get that. By the same token, I do believe that it can creep up on people. We all have vulnerabilities.

There have truly been times I feel I have no idea how I gained ten pounds, but if I look back, I can see every critical misstep along the way. My emotions skewed my ability to see it at the time, and it wasn't convenient to see what I didn't want to see.

Before my husband and I got married, we did some marriage prep, which included a questionnaire about beliefs and values. My husband asked me how I responded to one question in particular. The question was, "Would you leave your spouse if s/he cheated on you?" I told him that I responded, *no*. He asked why I responded that way. I told him that I believe all humans have the potential to be unfaithful and, knowing that, I could never say that I would *never* cheat because I am human. I don't intend to cheat. I don't want to cheat, but I can't promise that I would *never* cheat. Therefore, I could not hold another person to a higher standard than I believed possible.

He looked at me as if maybe he'd made a huge mistake in asking me to get married. He, of course, had responded that he would absolutely leave me if I cheated. In his world, everything fit into a neat box. We got married anyway.

I am a huge believer that we all have the shadow that

Carl Jung[9] talked about. It is a dark side—where we have the potential to do unsavory things. It is only when we deny and avoid our shadows that we are dangerous. I don't embrace my shadow, but I readily admit that it is there. I cannot manage what I pretend not to have or deny having.

Relationships get stale over time without work. It is very easy to find oneself vulnerable to attention from someone else. It may start out as a friendship, and as the connection builds, infidelity can occur seemingly without intent. In those situations, the unfaithful person made a decision-that was hurtful to someone else, but the problem existed within the relationship. The person who was unfaithful was a bad actor because of a bad situation. (Don't get me wrong. There are some bad actors out there who are just bad actors, but I am not talking about them.) All humans are temporary bad actors at some point in their lives.

Here is where the grit of risk comes into play. Once there has been infidelity in a relationship, the person who was cheated on asks, "Should I trust this person again? How can I? What should I do?"

I cannot answer these questions because they involve risks. All vulnerability involves risk. But in the case of infidelity, the risk is front and center. Should a person take a risk with another person who has been unfaithful? Is it worth it? It may be, but to do so absolutely involves courage.

Phyllis and Kenya came to see me in absolute turmoil. They had been married for ten years and had been together for fifteen. They described themselves as soulmates and best of friends. They had a quiet, comfortable life, although it was quite busy. They had two small daughters, ages three and five. Kenya worked from home part-time and was responsible for the kids' daily care. Phyllis worked as a communications director for a large corporation. Life seemed to get away from them as it does for many couples. They used to go on dates and carve out adult time, but life with kids happened. Weekends went way too fast. Kenya was exhausted from demands at home. Phyllis was exhausted from demands at work. They didn't fight a lot, but they just lost the connection.

Phyllis joined a softball league, and there she made some new friends. Kenya had even met some of them at a barbeque. Phyllis felt like Kenya was too busy with the kids to listen, so Phyllis started calling and texting a friend she'd made on the team. Before long, they were joking throughout the day and connecting. One thing led to another. Phyllis was having an emotional affair already, and then things got intimate. Kenya saw a text that didn't sit right with her. She got into Phyllis's phone and found more than she'd bargained for. She was devastated.

Phyllis and Kenya had a verbal fight like they'd never had before. It all came out—the resentments, the frustrations, the anger, and the hurt. Phyllis vacillated between absolute guilt and repentance to angry justification of her behavior. Kenya vacillated between soul-crushing anguish and destructive anger. They both, however, agreed to come to counseling.

At the outset, I explained that there were two separate issues. The first issue was the infidelity—healing around that. The second issue was the pattern of behavior that led up to the infidelity—and yes, they both played a part in that.

Generally, I find that couples appreciate my calm,

nonjudgmental attitude about infidelity. It helps them feel like they are *normal* (there it is again) and that it can be fixed if they choose that route. I also tell them that it is my policy to piss both people off equally if I am doing my job well. This is a shot across the bow that there is no one villain despite outward appearances. I also explain that the relationship can be saved if they are both committed to the work.

As is often the case, Kenya wanted me to tell her that if she stuck around, Phyllis wouldn't be unfaithful again. Kenya wanted to know undoubtedly if saving the relationship was worth it. She feared that she was being played. She felt like a fool for entertaining the thought of staying, but she couldn't bear to think of leaving. She felt some self-hatred for not being strong enough to just walk away. In Kenya's mind, she had a lot to offer. She never thought she'd put up with someone fucking around on her. She was a bad bitch who wouldn't stand for being treated this way. At the same time, she knew that Phyllis was more than someone who was unfaithful. They had a history. Kenya couldn't think clearly.

I could not tell Kenya that Phyllis would be faithful. I could only say that the relationship was worth exploring to see what could be salvaged.

The hardest issue was the one Kenya voiced next: "I find myself wanting to go through Phyllis's phone all the time. I want to read her emails. I want to follow her around without her knowing to see if she is where she says she will be. It's driving me crazy. I don't really want to stalk Phyllis, but I also do. After I check, I feel better for a little while, but then it all washes over me again. I feel I have to check again. I feel like it is all I am doing. I am obsessing and checking. I am losing my mind."

This is the really hard part to hear. When a partner cheats, it brings control issues to the forefront. Kenya mistakenly believed that if she monitored closely enough, she could catch Phyllis if she cheated again. Kenya mistakenly believed that if she caught the infidelity early, she would no longer be a fool. She would prevent herself from being hurt again. She would have rock-solid evidence to justify a decision to leave. Kenya was wrong.

If Phyllis was going to cheat again, Kenya could not prevent it. Why would she want to, anyway? Why would anyone want to *make* someone be faithful?

Kenya was giving up control of her life to the slavish task of stalking Phyllis. Kenya wasn't happy, and if she found out right away about any further cheating, it wouldn't hurt any less than the first time she'd discovered it. Telling herself that catching it early would save her pain was a lie.

I told Kenya that all any of us can do is focus on the evidence at hand—the evidence today, in this moment. None of us are guaranteed a future moment, anyway. We forget this. We operate as if we have forever. We all behave in ways that take others for granted. It is incredibly hard to remember to be in today, but it is doable.

If, today, Kenya believed her relationship with Phyllis was worth saving, and she committed to putting in the effort, then she had to adhere to her plan. She was saying aloud that she wanted to be in the relationship and wanted to move on, but the fact that she was always second-guessing and stalking undermined that. I typically tell people that if they do not or cannot trust the other person to be faithful, then there is no need to continue in the relationship. They have the answer they want. It is time to move on. If they say that they do trust, then they have to act like it.

No one—not one of us—has the ability to prevent being hurt. All relationships involve risk. If we put ourselves out there, there is a risk of being hurt. We do it because there is also a real payoff—that is, to find requited love. We cannot get there without risk. That risk is always there, but the hurt of infidelity highlights it.

Let me be clear, though: I am also not saying that every case of infidelity deserves taking a risk. In Kenya and Phyllis's case, it did, but in other cases, the relationship is beyond repair. When I talk about the grit of risk, I am talking about having the stomach to take a risk in situations where the risk is worth it. Of course, that is a personal decision. The problem is that I have seen people believe that the risk is worth it and still not allow themselves to take the risk.

In addition, I am not saying that all of the risk lies with the person who was cheated on, like Kenya. Phyllis does need to express remorse and make amends, and this involves risk too. There is the risk of admitting fault and trusting that the other person will not hold it over you until eternity. There is the risk of trusting that the hurt will pass and things will change. There is the risk of staying in a relationship that wasn't working and believing that it can work again.

I see folks like Phyllis become engulfed in feelings like guilt and regret. They react with anger to discussions of what happened, insisting that it is time to move on. They don't want to talk about it anymore. While I understand why they want this, it is not realistic. Discussion of what happened and how to prevent it in the future is critical. Talking about how to improve the marriage and ameliorate the conditions that led to the infidelity to begin with is likewise key. Forgiveness, though, is a journey, and both parties need to be patient. In the end, I tell folks that the more they focus on the infidelity, the more they invite the toxicity into the relationship. What happened happened. Process it. Understand it. Then, decide how you will use that information to move on.

There are no guarantees in life. Some things in life are worth the risk. Be smart, and figure out what those things are. Follow the evidence. Feelings are interesting data, but they are not always rational. They can take you to crazy places. Listen to your mind and your gut. They've got your back.

The grit of risk also involves trusting oneself. Sometimes infidelity really brings up self-doubt. People question their own decision-making, but what they don't immediately realize is that we never enter relationships with 100 percent certainty. It isn't possible. When infidelity happens, we jump to conclusions and negative self-talk about what we missed. We criticize ourselves for being poor judges of character, and it's all just a waste of time. The grit of risk is being in the moment and trusting ourselves to make the best decisions based on the available data at that moment. It is trusting ourselves to adjust as additional data become available, and it is giving in to the notion that risks of hurt also come with the risk of joy.

JOURNAL PROMPT

- What is your predisposition on trust of self and/or others, especially in ambiguous situations? Where does your sense of trust or distrust come from? What would you like to do differently in your life around trust?

Writing More about Your Grit

. . .

've tried to give you many examples of how I see grit present in the lives of real people. I find these examples gritty because they all involve showing up for the fight in life, having the courage to fight, and persisting despite all the barriers.

What stories resonated most and why? After reading this section, how has your idea of grit changed? How do you define grit?

Consider times in your life when you demonstrated grit under this broader understanding of what it can be. Write them down. What makes those times stand out?

What life experiences have helped you build grit or shaped your grit? How?

What strengths do you have that guide your grit? What challenges do you have around grit? What would you like to have more grit for?

Consider your self-talk and coaching style around grit. What things do you say to yourself that make your grit stronger? What do you say to yourself that makes your grit weaker? How can you do better?

How would you like to own your life experiences, strengths, and challenges and channel them into grit? What goals will you set? What is your plan? What will get in the way, and what will you do about it?

GROWTH

Growth is a part of life. We are either on the verge of growing, we are growing, or we are trying to avoid growing. Beyond that is death.

Growth covers everything I do in my profession because change is all about growth. I have seen people who resisted growing, and they became developmentally arrested or stuck. I have worked with people who grew and judged the direction as unacceptable. I have sat with people who were afraid to grow. I have also encountered loads of people who were chomping at the bit to grow past pain and unhealthy patterns.

The problem is what we are telling ourselves about growth. We label growth as good or bad. We tell ourselves things *should be* different and that things are *acceptable* or *unacceptable*. When we become trapped in the emotional quicksand of judgment, doubt, and fear, we get in our own way. This fucks up growth, and growth interruption is a developmental crisis that messes with all that will follow.

When we get in the way of our own growth by judging, it is a self-imposed crisis. The remedy is to become better objective observers of ourselves. We don't need to judge our growth. All change is growth. We don't need to call it good or bad. The important part is how we use it. What if we could become the wise sage in our own lives—the person who watches, waits, and reflects? Think about it for a minute. No one is a more knowledgeable expert on you than you, but emotions skew what you see and they get in the way of using the data in a productive way.

It's very hard to be an objective observer of yourself. It isn't a matter of just flipping a switch. It is a practice, but it is really stepping out of our own way. I call this knowing one's own bullshit, pointing at it, and saying, "There it is. There is the bullshit again. What do I want to do about it?"

This section on growth focuses on finding stillness and ways to step outside of ourselves to observe without reaction and watch the unfolding. It is about learning to say to ourselves, "I wonder what will happen next" with awe and curiosity and self-support.

I provide lots of examples of growth and note that it always involves pain. Showing up for a growth experience takes a lot of courage because often we're talking about deep-seated programming from childhood, mistaken beliefs, and fear of losing what we know. I guess that's why they're called growing pains.

JOURNAL PROMPTS

- When you think of major formative growth experiences in your life, what stands out? How did these experiences affect your growth? Did you get stuck anywhere along the way? How did you get unstuck?
- What has been your typical reaction to growth experiences? How do you tend to deny or avoid them, or do you embrace them more readily? What has stimulated your growth in the past?

- How do you measure personal growth? How do you include feedback from others?
- What are your initial reactions to growth opportunities, and what ones currently await you?

Slow-Healing Wounds

. . .

Eliza originally consulted me for family drama and conflict. It wasn't until we had been working together off and on for a few years that she told me that her older brother had molested her. I don't know if she had pushed it to the back of her mind hoping it would go away, or if she just wasn't ready to share it with me sooner. Either way, her saying it aloud was a bombshell because it made the experience real. There was no taking it back.

Eliza had been raised in a deeply religious family, and her family was well-known in their community. Her brother's behavior violated all of the very strict rules and teachings that had been in place when she was a child. Eliza was consumed with guilt and shame that deeply affected her function both inside and outside of the family. As she came to grips with the conflict in her family and within herself, she felt forced to confront the reality that her brother had sexually molested her for at least two years when she was around 12 to 13 years old. Eliza was incredibly distraught as she confessed the traumatic events because it became clear that she held herself responsible. She kept stating that she didn't know how she let it happen—as if it had been her responsibility.

This part of my work with Eliza took a full year to unpack. We talked about what happened and how it happened. We talked about how unfair it was for the adult Eliza to go back and judge the child as if she had the knowledge, the power, and the understanding to do anything but survive. We talked about the role of strict religious practice and the dominant elevation of men as the unquestioned authorities. We talked about how special attention of older figures can be confusing to kids, but none of this—*none of this*—was her fault. We talked at great length about her brother's damaged character and holding him accountable for the abuse he perpetrated.

We talked about the secondary trauma she was inflicting by blaming her younger self. It wasn't a fair fight. At times like this, I like to ask women if they would blame their younger daughters or sisters in the same position. The universal response is a horrified, "NO!" The point is made.

To further drive this point home, I often ask abuse survivors to find a photo of themselves around the time the abuse was occurring. I ask them to gaze into the eyes of the person in the photo and to empathize for a few moments. Then I tell them to imagine judging this child and imagine verbalizing the judgments to this child. This exercise tends to be incredibly powerful, and it enables folks to stop with the shame language.

During this year of intensive work, I saw Eliza grow from a highly self-questioning, uncertain young adult into her own person. While I cannot say that she was highly confident, she began to set boundaries that she'd never learned to set as a child. She began to protect herself the way no one had protected her before. This part was extremely painful as Eliza wondered if her mom, in particular, subconsciously knew about her brother and looked the other way because she didn't want to know. Although Eliza did not believe her mom directly knew of the abuse, she believed that her parents allowed it to happen within the family atmosphere they'd enabled.

Eliza also did a complete re-examination of her religious beliefs and the role they played in her subjugation to men.

For Eliza to transform into her own person, one who felt empowered to set boundaries and hold others accountable for bad behavior, she had to be truthful with herself. She also had to decide what she wanted to do with those truths going forward.

This part of counseling is an incredibly delicate time for individuals faced with the reality of a traumatic past, but they come to see that they have an active role in deciding what to do with it going forward.

I continued to see Eliza off and on over the next ten years. She struggled with her relationships with her family because she decided to keep the abuse private while also cutting herself off from her brother. She didn't want the toxicity of having him in her life, but she didn't want to get into the reasons with others she believed would not respect her trauma. Eliza's history was hers to share or not share. Although it was something that happened to her, it was not something that defined her.

Eliza learned to be the parent to herself that neither of her biological parents had been. She worked hard to develop self-confidence by *just doing it*. She went back to college and left an unhappy marriage. She found the hope to search for personal happiness as she defined it.

How did Eliza do these things? One day at a time, over many years. I recognize this answer is disappointing, but to describe how Eliza transformed herself and her life would be a book in itself. My point is that it can be done, and it takes time. I often see folks who want a prescription for how to grow and change with a timeline—like a medicine. How long will it take to kick in? It is frustrating that recovery from past trauma isn't that straightforward. Yet it is doable. I liken trauma work to daily stretching. You have to engage in the fundamentals every day, or you risk being tense and rigid. While you're stretching, you will become the expert on your experience. You will notice things. You work on what tensions surface in the stretch.

We all get frustrated that change doesn't happen overnight. We get a piece of insight and feel that it will change everything. While this insight does add to understanding, it doesn't change all the childhood brainwashing, habits, and social coercion that keep us from change. Change is a process that unfolds over time. It begins and ends with doing things differently and seeing things differently. It is a re-experiencing of the world under new circumstances or with new eyes.

Growth comes with pain. That is often how we know we're really growing. Sometimes we have traumatic pasts that interfere with growth, and we have to work harder. It takes longer. I want you to ask yourself: If your life is indeed about you being your best and living your best, aren't you worth all the effort? What could possibly be a better use of your time than working on you? The idea that working on yourself is a one-and-done proposition is a vicious lie. Growth is an unfolding. Each layer is another fold. Each moment is a new beginning.

JOURNAL PROMPT

- Think of something painful from your past. How did it affect or change you, and does it continue to do so? How have you grown or not grown?

Calling Out My Own Bullshit

. . .

I spend a lot of time helping people look inward at their personal contributions to problems because that is what they can control, but I understand that it is often our interactions with others that push us to painful moments of self-reflection. Others can stimulate "what is wrong with me?" feelings. In the end, it is still our own problem if we allow interactions with others to be a cancer on our psyche. It is all about noticing how we are feeling and deciding what to do with it, but we've got to catch it happening first.

I am human too. Even though I help others, I'm not immune to the pitfalls of being human. Here is one of my shining growth moments.

Reggie was a psychologist who wanted his own personal therapy for life stress. He'd had a lot of therapy in the past because he believed in practicing what he preached. He had seen several other providers over the course of many years and was ready to try someone new.

Reggie was in a group practice, and the partners were in the midst of a professional divorce. He worried about finances and was angry about perceived unfairness in the process. Going to work every day was not enjoyable. Reggie told me that he wanted therapy as a place to vent.

Anyone who has worked with me knows that I am not a good match for someone who *just wants to vent*. I do not see therapy as simply a place to vent. I see therapy as a place to work your ass off—reading and doing homework. I explained this, and Reggie was intrigued. He wanted to come back and see me, but he asked if he could spend the first couple of visits, at least, giving me his complete history.

Specifically, Reggie was asking for at least two visits for him to talk and for me to just listen. I perceived this to be a problem because Reggie had told me he'd already worked through his past in previous therapy. My style of therapy is not free-form, past-focused unless there is unresolved trauma from the past. Even then, my technique is more structured. I wasn't clear why Reggie and I would need a complete review. I also believed I had made my approach clear to Reggie.

Against my better judgment, I agreed. This was mistake number one. I changed my typical practice for one person in deference to his professional background. I didn't want to be seen as non-collegial. I also didn't want to feel rigid. I was overly concerned with what another health-care professional would think about me. I was overly concerned with pleasing and impressing one of my own.

I made an exception to my rules because I gave someone special status. Even typing this, I know it was wrong.

Reggie used a full three visits to detail all aspects of his childhood, bad relationships, abuse, educational experiences, and more. He wanted to give me the blow-by-blow even though it wasn't directly relevant to his current dilemma. Reggie believed I could not fully understand unless I knew everything. While I do believe that history is important, this felt different, too much. But once I opened that door, it felt hard to close. I silenced my discomfort and let things meander.

After extended listening, I was ready for action. I wanted to launch into skill-building, but each time I tried to teach a skill, Reggie said he already knew how to do that. It seemed there was nothing new to teach Reggie. I suggested reading, and he was inconsistent. Reggie had stated at the outset that he "just wanted to vent." I did not accept that at face value and pursued my own agenda. I was responsible for this dilemma.

Mistake number two was that I didn't call Reggie on his resistance and avoidance. I wanted to be respectful, and I worried that perhaps I indeed had nothing to offer this fellow professional. Internally, I knew this was bullshit. There is always something to learn. Perhaps I was too drawn into preserving my reputation, worried that Reggie might talk about me in professional circles. I again made an exception to my own rules for the wrong reasons.

Because Reggie already knew the skills I wanted to teach, and he couldn't discuss homework he hadn't done or found helpful, Reggie had plenty of time to *just vent*. See how that works?

After the venting, Reggie would tell me what valuable insight I'd provided—even though I'd said little. I felt good that a colleague would give me such a compliment, so I'd pat myself on the back while simultaneously feeling like I'd done something wrong. I knew I wasn't living my professional values, but I told myself that I was being flexible and thinking outside of my usual box. I was uncomfortable because I was lying to myself. See how that works too?

I'd work up the courage to confront Reggie about the fact that we weren't really working on goals, and this would go okay until he'd work into the conversation that he was disappointed in me or he somehow felt let down by something I'd said or done. Interestingly, he consistently felt disappointed in me on the days that I would do more than just let him vent. These episodes always caught me off guard, and it would take me a while to make sense of them. I would reflect on Reggie's feedback and wonder what I did wrong. I would strategize how to come at my concerns in a new direction. It should, after all, fall to me to find something therapeutic within his worldview.

It took way too long for me to recognize that Reggie was managing me. He praised me when I allowed him to vent, and he told me that I was not helpful—or worse, harmful—when I asked him to do more.

When I use the term *managing*, I simply mean people act in ways aimed to get what they want. It's not always a conscious process, and all humans do it from time to time. Typically, I'm very good at recognizing when people are managing me, but I was blind to this process with Reggie for a long time because I looked at him differently.

In the end, we always came back to Reggie venting, nothing changing, and me feeling irritable. I began to doubt myself when Reggie suggested that perhaps I had personal problems that interfered with our work together.

Oh shit. No, he didn't. Nothing messes with a therapist

more than suggesting the therapist is mixing personal issues with patient issues. He was really good at getting to me, and he was right. I had issues that were interfering, but they weren't the ones he thought.

I didn't want to be unaware. I reflected more. I consulted another colleague for guidance. No matter what I did, Reggie would maneuver the therapy visits back to straight-out venting. I was considering giving up, taking the money, and letting him vent freestyle . . . when Reggie dumped me. He told me that I wasn't helping him even though I'd tried. He said he felt judged by me. In the end, he told me that I didn't have the skills to provide what he needed. I wasn't able to provide the right therapeutic environment, which wasn't my fault, but it needed to be said.

At this point, I wasn't even offended. In fact, I laughed. It was all right there in front of me. I'd missed it because of ego, fear, need to impress. I was so relieved to not have to continue in discomfort that I didn't care.

As I said in the beginning, I am famous for reminding others that they control how they allow others to influence their feelings. I am not immune. Sometimes the problem is that we allow others to *make* us feel like we are the problems. We allow them to *make* us feel crazy. That part is on us.

I share this story to illustrate that even I am vulnerable to falling into this trap. No one is immune, but we must start with self-honesty. Growth cannot happen without self-honesty. When I made the exceptions for Reggie, I got caught in my need to impress him and made assumptions about him that were not based on actual data. I lied to myself, all the while knowing I was being dishonest. I didn't listen to my intuition. Growth is about being truthful with oneself and actually listening and acting upon authenticity.

My situation is worse than just being self-dishonest because I knew I was doing it while I was doing it. I just tried to talk myself out of it. This is highly disrespectful to gut instinct and never works, by the way.

Prior to Reggie, I would have told you that I was not into impressing others. This was a blind spot. We all have them. Growth is about paying attention so that when light is shone upon them, we see them.

When someone attempts to make you feel like you are crazy, the term is *gaslighting* (from the film *Gaslight*,[10] with Ingrid Bergman and Charles Boyer). Reggie did some of this, although I don't think he did it consciously. I think he did it to test people and to get what he felt like he needed—someone to listen. But no one should have to pay for someone to listen. That is what friends do for free.

People will gaslight. We cannot control that. What we can control is the part we play when we allow it to be effective. My gut told me that my situation with Reggie was going off the rails, but I ignored it. I often think of the gut as an extra sense that can tell us something is off when the brain isn't quite able to logically make sense of it all yet. We all need to listen to our gut and stop discounting it as being too picky or being overly sensitive or being judgy. It is there to tell us something.

Growth starts with self-integrity and ownership of what we do with the information. We all have the power to limit others' influence over our minds. We have to use it.

JOURNAL PROMPT

- Think of a time when you let your heart override your gut. Why did this happen, and what was the end result? What did you learn? What blind spots tended to be weaknesses for you, and what experiences contributed to your awareness around them?

Looking Beyond

...

The first time N'chelle contacted me, I was on high alert. If she hadn't told me that a former patient of mine referred her, I don't know that we'd have met at all. N'chelle's situation sounded like a hot mess before she called it one. On the phone, she launched into a long story about a shady romance, friends trashing her, conflict at work. I lost track of all the details on that initial call. Listening was like trying to drink from a firehose. I was overcome.

I mostly do brief therapy, preferring to see people off and on over their lives rather than weekly therapy over years. I was afraid that N'chelle wanted and needed more than my practice style allowed. However, at these times, I tell myself to keep an open mind. No one is calling me at their best.

I was on guard when N'chelle and I first met because I knew I had a series of questions to address during the visit, and I was afraid she'd talk my leg off. She was, however, very pleasant and easygoing. I found her answers to be succinct and on target.

I discovered that N'chelle was highly intelligent, with a well-rounded education. She was working a couple of different jobs, which demonstrated a strong work ethic. N'chelle was also an artist, and she shared some of her work with me. I was super impressed. She had a lot of talent.

I realized I could not have been more wrong in the conclusions I'd jumped to over the phone. N'chelle was, in fact, a very remarkable young woman, who presented as very thoughtful and together. It became clear, however, that her problems were relationship-based.

N'chelle described a traumatic childhood that involved persistent domestic abuse of her and her mother. N'chelle was the oldest child, and she often functioned as a mother to her younger siblings. She described her mom as passive and weak. Her father was domineering, abusive, judgmental, and authoritarian. N'chelle was a peacekeeper and caregiver at heart. She learned to walk on eggshells without breaking them, and she'd carried this skillset into her adult life.

In her romantic relationship, N'chelle's partner was not abusive, but she wasn't respectful either. There was a lot of gaslighting, subtle put-downs, and veiled threats of infidelity from the partner. N'chelle was surrounded with friends and family who always wanted or needed something. Very few of them were healthy and functioning, and N'chelle was at their beck and call for emotional first aid. Work was no better. Everyone dumped on N'chelle, and she was often blamed for anything that went wrong. She was a convenient scapegoat because she easily accepted blame—it was all she'd known.

All of this explained the whirlwind of our first phone conversation. N'chelle was reflecting the chaos of her environment.

N'chelle consulted me for perspective on getting her life in order, and she was blown away when I told her about boundaries. It amazes me when adults hear words like *boundaries* as if the concept is entirely novel. To N'chelle, it was 100 percent new information. Her father had brainwashed her to be a servant to those around her. She had no concept of loyalty to self. She had no concept of the right to refuse. As such, N'chelle never seemed to get anything done for herself. She was so consistently engaged in problem-solving and helping others that she never found forward momentum in her own life.

As we sorted this out, N'chelle marveled at the thought of doing what made her happy independent of everyone else. Indeed, it was as if hearing it from me was the first time she'd ever considered it. I was the first person she could remember telling her that she could and should do what made her happy. I was the first person who insisted that she owed it to herself to live up to her talent and potential and that every other person she knew was responsible for doing the same thing in their own lives without her helping them.

I explained to N'chelle that people had become dependent upon her and could not grow themselves as long as she was there to take responsibility for their problems. Of course, it would not be convenient to have to solve one's problems oneself, but convenience does not potentiate growth.

Ordinarily when I tell someone that they owe it to themselves to say no, this is not new information. They know this already, but they haven't felt able to do it or have felt guilty about doing it. With N'chelle, this was truly a light bulb moment. She'd never stopped to consider that saying no was an option.

Over the next several weeks, N'chelle started saying no. She said no to her partner's shenanigans. She said no to friends who tried to guilt her into dropping what she was doing to help them through another crisis. She said no to things she didn't enjoy. For every no, N'chelle said yes to herself. With her newfound time, she contemplated everything she'd done in her life and discovered it was always for someone else—even her career choices. N'chelle stopped to ask herself what made her happy and what she wanted to do with her life.

I'd catastrophized that working with N'chelle would be more than I wanted to handle. What I found was that once I told N'chelle that her life was her own, she didn't need me for very long. She flew on her own very quickly.

N'chelle mapped out an art career. She made a plan to achieve all the things she'd never had time for previously or things that others had pooh-poohed. N'chelle told me she felt free for the first time in her life. She felt alive. She felt wonderful. Yes, she did have a little guilt at first, but it didn't last nearly as long as she'd thought it would.

N'chelle was stuck developmentally, and together we simply removed the barrier, which was the perception that she was meant for no other purpose than to serve others who *needed* her. Remember that nothing external to N'chelle changed. What changed was the lens through which she viewed her life. N'chelle took responsibility for her own life and her own happiness, and doing so felt incredibly liberating.

We are all programmed to see the world in certain ways based on genetics and life experience. In this story, I point out my own programming flaws alongside N'chelle's. Our responsibility is to challenge that programming. Our responsibility is to own our own happiness. If we aren't happy, we are beholden to understand why and make a plan to do something about it. Feeling compelled to fix others' problems can be a prison, but just because we *feel* compelled doesn't mean that we *are* compelled to fix things. We always have a choice. The challenge is seeing the choice and framing the choice in reality. It isn't a choice between being selfish or selfless. It is really a choice of what we are responsible for controlling. Change starts with you.

JOURNAL PROMPT

- How have you sacrificed your happiness for others in the past and maybe even now? Why did you make the sacrifices, and were you intentional in doing so? What thoughts or feelings immediately jump to mind when I suggest saying no?

Be Where You Are When
You Are There

. . .

Sometimes I find myself feeling regretful about something from the past, but then I remind myself that the certain thing had to happen in order for me to learn a lesson, grow, or get to a different point. There is, however, a particular regret I have not been able to get past. That regret is when I haven't appreciated where I was at a particular time because I was so focused on being in the future.

Here is how my psyche reminds me of this: As a child, I lived next door to my grandparents, and I often played in both of our backyards, because it gave me a lot of space to run. As an older child, I had this recurring dream that there was a secret park way in the back of my grandparents' yard. No one else could get there, and I had to be in just the right spot to see it. It was as if the park existed in another dimension, and conditions had to be just right for me to be able to get there. I could step into the park by approaching it a certain way, and sometimes I couldn't find it at all. No one else knew it existed. I had a wonderful, warm euphoria associated with this dream, so much so that I would often go in search of the park during my waking hours. I never found it.

There were even times in my dreams when I would go to the part of the yard where the park was, and I was not able to find it. I would wake feeling sad and empty.

I believe this dream is related to sadness about growing up. As a child, I adored playing freely with kids in my neighborhood, especially at the park. At the same time, I was in a big hurry to grow up. As much as I wanted to grow up and move on from childhood, there was also something magical about it—probably the lack of structure and order and true freedom without judgment. I can recall having this dream even as a young adult and feeling so wonderful every time I had it. I still had the urge to return to the backyard in search of the park. As I grew into adulthood, that dream eventually died away.

Late in my twenties, I was steeped in graduate school, which I now identify as one of the happiest times of my life. I was surrounded by some of the most giving, fun, and supportive people I have ever known. Every day I got to learn the most fascinating theories and ideas. I got to learn from the most remarkable experts. At the same time, I was always struggling with a lack of money. There was much I wanted to do, but I could not afford to do most of it. I was ready to get on with my life and make some money. I couldn't build anything permanent until I moved on from graduate school. My mind was in the future again.

I spent my last year of graduate education on an internship in the Deep South, away from family and friends. This was an incredible time. I lived alone and knew no one before moving there. This was never something I would have done earlier in life, and it was a true sign of how much I'd grown. I met great people during this year, and I learned to really enjoy being alone. At the same time, I had plenty of visits from friends, and we had amazing adventures.

I have a couple of recurring dreams about these grad school days. I dream that I somehow magically find myself back in the company of everyone from grad school. I am bathed in the laughter, joy, and comfort of seeing old friends, most of whom I have not seen since school days. The other persistent dream is similar, but I find myself back in this Southern city. I dream that I have arranged a girls' trip there. All the women are able to come, and we head off to this *secret* street in the city that no one knows about—because it doesn't exist in waking life. It has all these amazing restaurants that I have been to but not been able to visit in years. This dream street is one that very few people know about, and like my dream park, it can only be found by approaching it at a certain angle. All the women are thrilled with delight to be able to get back there and share in the memories.

I wake up from these dreams in real tears. Though the dreams are filled with laughter and joy, at some level I am aware that they are not real, and I am weeping with sadness and nostalgia. My heart misses the people, the places, and amazing memories that I cannot possibly relive.

The secret park. The secret street. They represent sacred parts of my life.

As I say all of this, my life is wondrous. I have great adventures. I am surrounded by beautiful people. I am truly happy. However, I am acutely aware that nothing will stay the same. Everything is changing as it is happening. I try very hard to be present during this time and appreciate every moment.

This lies beneath my regret. While I was immersed in some of the most wonderful times of my life, I now feel I didn't fully appreciate what I had when I had it because I was overly focused on what I did not have or where I wanted to go next. When we are not fully present where we are at the time, we miss out on the fact that the clock is always ticking. Things are always changing. The things we want often come in time, but when we are hyper-focused on having them now, we miss what is right in front of our very eyes.

This process of being aware of what is happening while it is happening is called *mindfulness*. It is about being fully present in that moment. Underlying this is a strong ability to be patient that what we want to change will eventually happen. Patience is a quality I have found to be pervasively challenging for most human beings.

I don't know of any cool trick that will make being mindful easy or obvious. I can only say that it is so easy to fall into the trap of being future-oriented, particularly when there is something unpleasant about our present circumstances. Many people use mindfulness meditation, which is a fabulous skill and practice. However, I haven't been able to convince many people to stick with it, even myself.

As I write this, we are smack in the middle of the coronavirus pandemic, and there is little about this time that I would call ideal. Far from it. So many things are painful, yet at the same time, things are as they are. If we try to skip ahead past the pain, we will miss some very important information. I try to remind myself that there will come a day when I long to be at home with my teenagers, having them all to myself. I will long for the feeling of being together watching movies on end and getting on each other's nerves.

I don't mean to say that we should enjoy or appreciate painful times like this. What I am saying is that we are here, and much of being here is what we make of it. There are always things to be learned. The pain can just be pain, or it can instigate growth that will create positive change in our lives and the world. If we ignore the things we believe to be ugly or unacceptable, we cannot find ways to fix them.

Being present is a practice. I purposefully catch myself jumping ahead and remind myself to look around. We are where we are for a reason. Instead of fighting it, I am trying to appreciate it a little more because change is guaranteed, and I will never be able to rewind that clock to get a second chance or better look. This is growth.

JOURNAL PROMPT

- The mind is prone to reviewing the past and fretting about the future. We want to escape present pain. What have these patterns cost you as you reflect more deeply? How would you like to begin to cultivate a present mindset in your life, and why?

Watch Like a Spectator

. . .

One of the reasons I love my job so much is that I meet extraordinary people who teach me extraordinary life lessons. I owe so much of my growth to the people who consult me.

Lizzie is one of those people.

Lizzie came to see me on the recommendation of her physician for strange medical symptoms with no explanation. It is not unusual for me to see people with unexplained medical problems, and I tend not to jump to conclusions that a person's concerns are solely of a psychiatric nature. This is part of the human experience. Medicine cannot explain everything, and there are times we show stress, anxiety, and grief in the body. Who is to know?

I can't tell you the number of times that I have had weird bodily symptoms—especially digestive—that drive me crazy. So, I call the physician, but by the time I get there, my symptoms have disappeared. We all have physical signs of stress in our bodies. There is absolutely no way to say that something is all in the mind or all in the body. What does it hurt to have an open mind? Things eventually reveal themselves.

My role isn't to determine whether people are faking. My role is to help people better manage stress because stress may present as physical symptoms or even make physical symptoms worse. My role is to meet people in their reality and work within that reality.

Regardless of my approach, Lizzie wasn't excited to see me. She felt like she was being sent to the *headshrinker* (as she called me) to *get her head shrunk* (as she called it).

Lizzie's situation was tough in many ways. I could see in her eyes that she'd had a difficult life. In addition to Lizzie's symptoms not making obvious sense, she was pursuing a lawsuit based on them. She didn't feel believed or understood by her treatment team. Psychologists know that when lawsuits are involved, it becomes extremely complicated. Lawsuits are stressful, they reinforce the sick role, and there are financial incentives. Attorneys openly call patients liars. Private investigators get involved. Lawsuits cause illness.

None of this means that lawsuits are improper. It just means that lawsuits complicate matters. It also means that other people will question if the symptoms being litigated are real. I told Lizzie that I didn't care about the lawsuit or whether her symptoms were real or not. I asked her to tell me about her life.

Lizzie said she had a horrible childhood. She asked if we could skip it because she didn't feel like discussing it. When I asked if she had experienced abuse, she made it clear that her whole life included abuse. We left it there.

Lizzie looked older than her stated age. She had the eyes of a woman who'd seen hell and lived to tell the story. She looked tough, too, like someone you wouldn't want to mess with. Despite her physical ailments, I felt she could kick my ass if necessary.

I asked Lizzie to give therapy a chance so that perhaps I could teach her some ways to manage her stress. I said, "What do you have to lose other than time?" She agreed to show up and give it a try, and she was interactive. At the same time, Lizzie enjoyed throwing out provocative comments to see what I would say. Because I knew she was looking for a reaction, I generally responded as if it were a normal conversation. I gave no clue to any shock I might have felt.

I suspected Lizzie was testing me, and that was okay. I surmised that she'd been hurt too often in the past. It was okay to not trust me.

One day, Lizzie came in, and I was about to launch into teaching mode. She said she needed to make better eye contact and that her eyes weren't working well that day. She got up, crossed the room, and sat right on my lap. She looked me in the eye and said, "So I can see you better."

I want to pause here to say that this had never happened to me and has not happened since. While I was taught during training that touch should be limited and purposeful, I was never taught what to do if a patient came and sat on my lap.

I did not feel threatened. I did not feel like Lizzie was coming on to me sexually. It felt like a test.

Thank goodness I had been in practice a long time and knew about mindfulness. My first reaction was to pause internally and wonder, *what the hell is going on here?*

Since I wasn't being threatened, I did not react. I've got a decent game face for these situations. When I reflected, I knew that the purpose of the behavior was to provoke me. What Lizzie had done to this point was not working. She had to up her game. She was testing me. What would I do? Would I reject her like others? Would I become violent? Would I kick her out? Would I re-create the fucked-up dynamics that she experienced in other relationships? Could Lizzie trust me?

Instead of reacting, instead of playing into what Lizzie expected, I did nothing. I caught myself starting to judge the situation (wondering what my colleagues would think or if this was going to get me into trouble), and thought to myself, *what the hell? Let's see where this goes. This has never happened to me, and it could be interesting.*

I said to Lizzie that although I'd been trained to not be so close to patients, if she felt more comfortable listening on my lap, so be it. I launched into my lesson on cognitive-behavioral therapy techniques with her on my lap. Eventually, she got up and moved.

I'm a pro at taking the fun out of situations. It's called being a mother.

Lizzie started calling me "Yoda" after this visit. And, you know what? It felt like a sign of respect. I also gained a deeper respect and appreciation of Lizzie.

I would like to wrap this all up in a nice, neat bow, but I cannot do that. I saw Lizzie for the number of visits that she agreed to at the outset in order to appease her physician. She was not healed at that point. She still had her initial symptoms, and that doesn't surprise me because there were too many things that were unresolved.

Lizzie's outcome is not the point of the story. The point of the story is that others are not responsible for our reactions. We are responsible for our reactions. If we suppress our knee-jerk reactions, we never know where it might lead. All of the judging and reacting can get in the way of allowing things to unfold.

This story is also about having an open mind. When we become reactive and shut uncomfortable encounters down, we close off opportunities to learn and grow.

Earlier in my career, I would have dreaded seeing someone with unexplained physical symptoms because I would see that person as hard to treat. A person who is hard to treat really means a person who doesn't cooperate in the way we want or who doesn't get better. It seems to be the ultimate insult—a patient who doesn't respond well to treatment, as if they do it on purpose.

At some point I recognized that I was taking how a person responded to therapy too personally. Whether or not someone gets better or not is not on me. It is on that person. I am not a deity. I can assist with healing, but I don't bestow it on people.

If a person is difficult to treat, it is a sign of the difficulties they face. Whether or not the person gets better is not a reflection of my worth. In addition, I was measuring my effectiveness based only upon the response I sought to see. Often, we don't even see the effect we have on other people. It is hidden.

Before I understood all of this, it was as if I were taking a person's condition or behavior as a personal failure or rejection. It's the same thing as being offended if someone didn't get better as I commanded. Having a mindful outlook is about seeing where it all will lead.

Growth is about stepping back, not judging, and watching to see how things unfold. Growth is about observing what will happen next.

This lesson reminded me that not everything is about me.

And sometimes it leads to so many more interesting places.

Do or don't do. That is on you.

JOURNAL PROMPT

- What particular things do you get judgmental about? How does that judgment affect your growth?

Growth Doesn't Follow the Charts

. . .

I remember when Sydney came to see me for the first time. She was a teen, and her mom brought her in after a conversation they'd had about sexual orientation. Sydney's mom asked her if she was gay. Sydney told her that yes, she felt attracted to other women even though she hadn't dated anyone. Sydney lived in a very small, conservative community. It was not safe to be out. Sydney's mom wanted her to talk with a professional to be sure she was okay.

Sydney was well-adjusted, talkative, and pleasant. I asked about her likes, her social and school activities, and her friends. Overall, it seemed like Sydney was doing quite well. I didn't find anything concerning in the history she provided.

I approached the visit as preventative, which means I wanted to use the opportunity to give Sydney education that might help her navigate challenges in the future. I spent some time educating Sydney on developmental models of sexual orientation to help her think about where she was in her self-acceptance. Sydney was mostly quiet, but she listened. We talked about how to be safe in choosing with whom she shared her sexual orientation in her community.

Although I felt I had connected well with Sydney, she did not return to see me after the first visit. I told myself that it was fine because she probably didn't need further counseling after all. Sydney had good social and family support. She was fine.

Except she wasn't.

Sydney came back to see me a few years later to talk about her sexual orientation, self-esteem, and happiness. As a part of our reintroduction, Sydney told me that she never returned to see me after the first visit because she thought I might have been homophobic.

I was completely dumbstruck. I didn't know what to say. I asked Sydney what I said that contributed to her feeling that I was homophobic. She stated that when I was talking about the sexual orientation model, she got spooked. She told herself that I must have been homophobic because the interaction felt awkward to her. Sydney stated that she knew I was not homophobic and that at the time she had, in fact, projected her own homophobia and discomfort onto me. Because she did not accept herself, she imagined that I had not accepted her either. She was now ready to confront her sexuality and work through her relationship fears.

We all do this. We take our fears and insecurities and convince ourselves that is how others see us, how they feel about us, and what they think about us when, in fact, it is only how we feel about ourselves. We take ambiguous looks and words and attribute negative beliefs. We assume that others won't like us because we don't like ourselves.

When I talk about filters, this is what I mean. The way in which we see the world is colored by our own beliefs and experiences. We see things through our own lenses, which may be distorted. All we can do is know this, catch this, and challenge this to be sure our perceptions are accurate.

Sydney also wasn't ready to confront some of the issues I presented. She just wasn't ready, and that's okay. She knew where I was when she was ready. This is growth. It can happen gradually. It can happen in spurts. Growth happens as we allow it, based on our readiness.

My experience with Sydney also reminds me that at any moment, each of us has a world of other things going on that others don't know about. We can look at others and assume that they have it so good or handle things so well when, in fact, they are struggling. We can assume that crazy drivers are careless jerks when maybe they are racing to a sick loved one or to the emergency room. We jump to conclusions that others have bad intentions or lack manners when there is so much more that we don't know about.

Our minds constantly seek to fill in blanks with data that fit our own worldview. Growth is about expanding our worldview and challenging long-standing biases.

So many people with anxiety tell me that they are flooded with fear of embarrassment in social settings because they become preoccupied with what others are thinking about them. I kid them, "Get over yourself! Seriously, do you really believe that everyone you meet is focused on you? Who are you thinking about? Yourself! Exactly. That is what we are *all* thinking about." So, when you conclude that everyone in the room is thinking how hideous you look, you are simply tormenting yourself. They are likely thinking about how *they* look or that they'd rather be somewhere else.

I do understand the idea that if we think the worst of someone else, we can protect ourselves from hurt, but this is a flawed assumption. I am not clear how thinking the worst of others helps at all. It just doesn't work. What it does do is put us in shitty moods. We can spend all day every day being pissed off, but it is not clear to me how that helps, other than to ruin our own days. We can choose better.

JOURNAL PROMPT

- How do you personalize what goes on around you? What are your patterns? What role does mind-reading play in your life and relationships? What thoughts or feelings do you tend to project onto others?

Own Your Shitshow

...

Louisa came from a super-religious family. She was raised to have very clear ideas of right and wrong. She believed that her every move was being judged and was fearful that she would be punished if she made the wrong choices in life.

Louisa spent most of her free time during childhood in church-related activities. She and her family went to church three times a week, were active in church socials, and were leaders in the church community.

Louisa's parents instilled in Louisa a belief that she must always be on guard because others are watching, just like God. What others thought of her was very important. Louisa was encouraged to wear her hair a certain way, dress a certain way, and talk a certain way. Her parents tightly controlled her friend group, social activities, and exposure to pop culture.

Although there were times Louisa wondered about the rigidity of her life compared to the lives of her peers, she was too afraid to confront it—until she went to college. At first, she was terrified of the freedom she experienced, but she was also intrigued.

Over time, Louisa came to believe that her upbringing was over-the-top *wrong*. She wanted to find a middle lane that allowed her to feel less judged. However, she struggled to find this middle lane. Louisa had married and had three daughters, but she'd gotten divorced. Her mom never let her forget about it.

Louisa found herself being driven to visually present as well-put-together. In other words, she had to dress neatly and have her hair just so. She judged herself constantly for being a bad mother. She caught herself encouraging her daughters to be overly concerned with what they were wearing even for simple things like a Target run. Louisa felt driven to keep the house spotlessly clean and organized, but she felt like she mostly failed at this.

While Louisa didn't want to act in these ways, she felt compelled by standards beyond her control.

Life itself was messy. Louisa's ideas of perfection never seemed to come to fruition. The dog got to the food on the table and pulled it off. She got messages from teachers that one daughter was the class clown and needed discipline, and another daughter was close to failing several classes. Louisa worked full-time and could never keep up with laundry and housework.

Louisa felt guilty that her kids played video games and ate junk food, even though she knew these activities were normal among other kids their age. There was the difference between knowing with the head and feeling with the heart.

Family gatherings were highly stressful because Louisa had developed new beliefs that conflicted with her parents'. She hated the way her mom would come over and criticize her cooking, her lifestyle, the way she looked. At the same time, Louisa doubted herself. She struggled to find her voice with her mom because she didn't want to come off as disrespectful. She often just took the criticism without comment, but Louisa was becoming bitter and angry.

Louisa started reading self-help blogs online and decided to check out therapy. Louisa had never considered therapy as an option because her parents taught her that therapists would put secular ideas in her head.

In therapy, Louisa surprised herself at how much anger and frustration flowed out of her, and then she felt overcome with guilt for saying those negative things aloud.

Louisa was relieved when I finally got to talk and told her that it was normal to feel that way. She was normal. It was clear to me that Louisa had never heard that. She'd only heard that all of the things about her were sinful and in need of improvement. It was as if Louisa didn't possess an internal compass to realistically evaluate herself. She'd never developed the ability to know how she was doing without external feedback, which was always negative anyway.

I told her that all of the perfectionism was something her parents had taught her. We talked about how those early life experiences were crystallized into very rigid and harsh standards and self-talk. Over time, I encouraged Louisa to own her shitshow as okay just the way it is.

Owning your shitshow is about giving yourself permission to be happy with life as you make it—regardless of what others are doing or what they think. You aren't living your life for others. The more she ran from it or tried to make it into something she could not control, the more out of control Louisa felt. I explained that everyone has a shitshow. Absolutely everyone. It is not possible to be without one.

I asked Louisa, "If it is what it is, why do you need to judge it?" The judgment piece was under her control, while much of the rest was not. The judgment only made it worse. It was as if Louisa had never before considered this. I asked, "Who cares what your kids look like in the store? Seriously! Do you have time to care about what other people are doing and judge it? Similarly, they don't have time to judge you. What difference does it make anyway?"

While the emotional learning of childhood wasn't going to disappear, Louisa learned to challenge it. She gained the tools to own her shitshow rather than run from it, deny it, cover it up. Being authentic was not only more likable but also more freeing.

Many people ask me how this kind of change occurs. The answer will be unsatisfactory. It is about seeing yourself repeating unhealthy patterns, paying attention to how and when this happens, and doing anything you can to interrupt the typical response. It is about practicing self-awareness, owning your reactions, and arguing the mistaken beliefs and negative self-talk that drive your old behaviors. It is repetitively hard work.

Louisa could give herself that permission any time, and she needed to stop waiting for others. Part of this involved boundaries. Louisa had to develop boundaries with herself—when to back off from others and when to tell others to back off. Respectfully telling her mother to stop critiquing was not being rude and was, in fact, healthy. Louisa had to learn that she set her own boundaries because it was crazy-making to let others set them for her. If others decided for her, she'd have to change herself to fit each set of expectations in every situation. There would never be consistency.

In some respects, Louisa had to learn her own standards, which is generally a task initiated in adolescence. It is about being comfortable with being genuine and authentic and validating your own experience as important.

Sometimes we don't grow according to the textbook schedule, but it's never too late to start. The trick is owning how you choose to grow and allowing it to happen without judgment. Better late than never.

JOURNAL PROMPT

- What role modeling did you have around judgment and boundaries? What was the legacy of that role modeling in your life? Flag some areas where you might need to set better boundaries with yourself and others so you can own your personal shitshow.

Black and White

. . .

will never forget my psychology internship. After five years of closely supervised practice and coursework, psychology interns apply for one year of paid clinical work experience. In my day, veteran treatment facilities were *the* place to train. Some of the best of the best clinical teachers worked there. These facilities paid well for internships, and there were tons of patients with a lot of problems to discuss.

I chose to work in the Deep South, and it changed me forever. I met people who changed my whole way of looking at life. They changed my being. I will forever be indebted to the men (because men were my only referrals while there) who allowed me the privilege of knowing them and working with them. I am also forever indebted to the training faculty who were real, fallible people who allowed me to make my own mistakes.

I don't want to make the veteran treatment facilities sound like some kind of oasis; there is much they can do to improve in terms of providing quality health care. But as far as my experience in the provision of mental health services, it was amazing.

I could also talk about many different people I worked with, but I want to focus on Bud. I have never known anyone like Bud, and I probably never will again.

By way of background, I am extremely White. I grew up in rural Southern Illinois where most people were White. I attended Eastern Illinois University (in the middle of farm country), and all my friends were White. I don't even recall encountering many people of color, to be honest. I was so White that this never even struck me as odd.

I learned in graduate school that this was White privilege. I didn't even know what White privilege was at that time, which is what makes it White privilege. I realize that some White people may react negatively to the term "White privilege." I understand. By objective standards, I grew up in a family with very limited financial resources, and I was the first person in my family to attend college. I wouldn't call my background privileged. To folks who have had significant life challenges, privilege may seem an ill-fitted word. At the same time, I can honestly say, I never, ever gave a second thought to my skin color or how it might affect others' perceptions or treatment of me. This is indeed a privilege that coexisted with other challenges I faced while not negating them. I will leave it at that, and I hope you will finish this story even if you feel reactive to that term.

I went to Indiana State University in Terre Haute for graduate school, and I began to meet people who were not White and who were not heterosexual (another identity I was oblivious about). There were not a lot of folks different from me, but there were some. I was sometimes shocked by differences, but I tried to keep an open mind. I was always worried about appearing to be the local hick. I projected a persona of comfort when I was often completely on edge.

I was on edge because I didn't want to say or do the *wrong* things. There were times I literally didn't know how to act because I doubted everything I knew. I also wanted to show that I was accepting. When I became aware of White privilege, I felt even more awkward. To make matters worse, I believed that I couldn't speak about any of this because I was too afraid of being seen as a racist. I was clueless about my own racial biases and stereotypes.

Looking back, this was all part of my journey. As if I could fake it.

I got through and even made a few casual Black friends. At the time, I called all my Black friends African American because I thought that was being respectful. In fact, I didn't truly understand the differences among Black people.

Then I moved to the South. I got an apartment in the inner city. I loved the city. It felt vibrant. It had character. My family told me it was scary and unsafe. I felt uncomfortable sometimes, but I was also excited. It was unlike anything I'd ever experienced.

New psychology interns were assigned long-term patients to see on a regular basis for a full year. If one of the relationships ended early, we would get a new one, but again, the plan was long-term. All my patients were people of color.

One patient, whom I saw for the entire year, was Bud, and he was Black.

Bud was much older than me. He came to every visit dressed to the nines. He would have a fancy derby hat and always wore a different suit. The suits were not what I had experienced as typical—brown, black, or gray. They were all colors, and he often paired them with vibrant shirts. Bud's shoes were polished and equally eye-catching. He also used a lot of cologne, and I could always smell him coming and going.

Bud was flamboyant. He walked with an obvious strut. He had a bounding voice, and he used wildly colorful language regardless of setting or audience.

Bud was a veteran with a very long medical record. I couldn't even get through it all. He had years and years of psychiatric visits with multiple providers. He had a long list of diagnoses. He had a long list of medications. All of this told me that Bud brought a lot to the agenda.

By this point, I had been educated on why vets struggle.

They see a lot of shit go down. Some generations fought wars they—and society as a whole—didn't and perhaps still don't understand. They may have been exposed to chemical agents with devastating, life-threatening, and life-ending aftereffects. Some told me they were asked to engage in perceived atrocities and were given access to drugs and alcohol to numb it all. In the past, vets have returned to a nation that shamed and rejected them. They have not always been celebrated as heroes. They haven't all gotten parades.

To top it all off, many vets have had traumatic lives prior to entering the military. What we know about trauma is that it builds upon itself—meaning that if I have childhood trauma, any trauma I experience after that mixes with past traumas. This is why it is important to better screen for trauma among military combat candidates. We know that some people will likely not ever recover from additional traumatic events.

I got the impression that there was a time that the military would take anyone to send into battle. I saw veterans who had no business being in the service because they did not have the capacity to understand what they were doing.

Add to all of that the open racism experienced within the military and American society.

When Bud and I met for our first counseling visit, he went into a diatribe about how *once again* he was being fucked over by the government. He was being assigned to a *White student.* He felt shafted, less than.

I couldn't blame Bud. I was a newbie who had never worked with veterans. I had very little experience with other cultures. If I were Bud, I wouldn't have wanted to see me either.

I wasn't offended, but I was intimidated and afraid. Bud was a big, loud Black man. I was a five-foot-tall, 125-pound White woman.

Yes, all of those stereotypes were triggered for me. I am human.

Plus, I worked in a clinic where folks acted out at times. When you combine substance use, long waits, financial stress, bureaucracy, and a short fuse, it is not surprising.

Upon starting at the treatment facility, the interns had training on how to protect ourselves in violent situations. Not long before I started, an intern was walking through the waiting room when a patient grabbed the lanyard around her neck and started choking her. We were told not to wear lanyards and were trained in self-defense. It created the impression that things got dicey in the clinic.

Then, Bud said it. He said—to my face—"I hate White people." Luckily, Bud liked to talk, and he used up most of the visit telling me about all the ways he'd been screwed over in life culminating in this moment, being assigned to the new White student, whom he hated already.

Thinking back, I don't recall anyone of color being available to see Bud even if he had been reassigned.

Up to this point, I'd heard a lot about racism, but I had never knowingly witnessed hatred being expressed so openly. I was basically ignorant of a lot of racism that I'd likely seen covertly. I was one of those people who was always shocked to hear about racist experiences, thinking, *Oh, this must not happen these days around here in Indiana.* I was that level of clueless in my White privilege. It was shocking to hear someone overtly express hate for me based on my race.

I was trained in Rogerian therapy. This meant that I was trained to provide unconditional positive regard and acceptance. I was trained to listen, validate, and understand. So, I did that to the best of my ability. I accepted that Bud had some terrible experiences in life that led to this moment, and it was my job to learn more. I understood that Bud could not hate me yet. He'd just met me. Give that some time. I must have done well at this because Bud decided to come back and see me again after that first visit.

In fact, I saw Bud almost every week for the entire year of my internship. I learned about Bud's abusive childhood. I heard about Bud's horrific wartime experiences. I heard about Bud's ongoing family drama and hardships. Bud told me that he slept with a gun by his bed, and sometimes he would put it in his mouth. I lost sleep worrying about Bud.

I had never met anyone like him, and to this day I have not ever worked with anyone else so volatile.

At the end of that year, Bud and I both cried. He told me that I was the best therapist he'd ever had. I told him that it was the privilege of my life to work with him. I would never forget him. I told him that I loved him, and he said it back to me.

To be clear, I was not the best therapist, but I listened and learned. I accepted. I tried not to judge. I cared, and perhaps most importantly, I validated his experience as real. Maybe that was more than Bud had ever had. Perhaps others bought into the machismo he used to push them away. I'd passed a few tests.

People are not always as they initially seem. We judge by appearance, expectations, biases, stereotypes. We don't always give people a chance to show us what is inside. When I first met Bud, I was not excited about the match. Clearly, he was less excited than I was.

Bud saw me through the lens of the discrimination he has experienced his entire life. I saw him as someone so different from me that I could never understand. We were both wrong.

I can only speak to my own lessons, which were many.

I now prefer overt statements that call out stereotypes and discriminatory attitudes because when they are hidden, I don't know that they are there. When I moved to Michigan, I tried to discuss race with patients, but no one wanted to talk about it. In the North, I guess, it is considered taboo or rude, or perhaps Black people are too afraid of being honest about fears. In the South, they just say it outright. I prefer that, but I realize that it takes a naked honesty with oneself to know those biases. I don't think society takes inventory enough.

We all have biases and stereotypes. It is how the brain is wired. It is a way we become more efficient. We create categories to describe. The problem is that not everyone fits into a category, or just one category. Humans can't help the way the brain is wired. What we can help is working at ongoing self-awareness so that we can manage these stereotypes and biases. We can work to ensure that we are exposing ourselves to people, ideas, experiences, and cultures that are different from our own.

What drives me so crazy in our current divisive discourse about race is when people claim there is no discrimination—no bias. There will always be some sort of bias because it is a flaw in human nature, and we have to acknowledge it to find a better way to manage it.

I also hate the over-the-top political correctness that leaves folks feeling like they can't make mistakes. Sure, some of this has to be owned, but a hyper-righteous tone can be unhelpful.

More than anything, we need to be able to have a conversation about different experiences and respect that each person—even if they are of our own ethnicity—may have had a different experience. We all have unique backgrounds and lenses through which we see the world, and we can't box those up or label them all as the same as others. Not all Black people want to be called African American. It is okay to ask how a person identifies. I have been surprised at the responses when I've asked.

This is why *color blindness* doesn't work. I get the overall idea, but it is too simplistic. To be color-blind negates all that is special and different, and in the end, we do not need to fear difference.

We need to take risks. My risk is sharing this story. I am far from being an expert in diversity. The fact is that I would never have chosen to work with this explosive character, Bud. I would have been too afraid. I would have been afraid because of stereotypes but also because of a fear of saying or doing the wrong thing. We are sometimes so polite and worried that political correctness gets in the way of honesty and curiosity. That is fear.

In the end, it is difference that will allow us to survive as a society. Difference can be scary, but learning about differences can take us to a new level of self-understanding that makes the world so much more beautiful and interesting.

It takes an open mind, and fear closes that mind. Fear intimidates. Fear gets in the way. Fear shuts down curiosity. Fear strangles ideas and growth. Fear prevents us from really knowing one another.

Growth cannot happen unless we face down fear. Bud taught me that fear of difference is not rational. I hope that I taught Bud that love can be found in the most unexpected places. We taught each other that despite differences, we are all human and share vulnerabilities, hopes, and heartaches.

JOURNAL PROMPTS

- Think of a time when you faced someone or something different that caused you to feel vulnerable or uncomfortable. How did you handle it? How did it change you? What did you learn?

- This story may bring up some powerful emotions around racial identity and racial differences. Write about your reactions. Reflect on these. Give these thoughts and feelings some space. Talk to someone or read the words of someone with a different perspective. Write more.

Writing More about Your Growth

...

Growth encompasses everything about being a human. It is my hope that we are all growing all of the time. The hard part is owning it and deciding *how* we are growing. This takes a lot of energy and thought.

Get out a piece of paper, turn it horizontally, and draw a line across the entire paper. At the beginning of the line, write the year of your birth. At the end of the line, write the current year. Make hash marks along the line to denote the most significant growth experiences of your life, both positive and negative events.

Write about major life events that have affected your growth. Describe the effects. Describe how the effects have influenced the ways you have seen the world and interacted with others.

While you can't go back and rewrite history, you can actively influence the sense you make of the past. How do you want to begin to own your growth experiences and feed your grit?

I want you to specifically consider pain here. What events in your life came with a lot of pain or discomfort?

How did you handle them? What is your typical response to pain? After reading this section, how would you like to approach pain differently?

What do you think of the idea of becoming an observer of yourself and your growth without judgment? How can you better facilitate this? What gets in the way? What will you do about it?

HOPE

H ope can be a hard word to define. According to Dictionary.com,[11] hope is the feeling that things will improve or change, but I am not sure that this definition captures all that hope is. To me, hope is more than a feeling. It is a sense of confidence that the future will be better based on certain beliefs about what is going on. In essence, I see hope as a feeling but also a belief or set of beliefs.

Jerome Groopman, MD, author of *The Anatomy of Hope*, describes hope as a feeling common to the human experience even if an accurate description escapes us. He believes that hope is not simply optimism or positive thinking but instead the feeling that comes from seeing something better in the future.[12]

Dr. Groopman sees hope as essential to human existence. Without hope, it seems there is no purpose. I often ask about hope when I meet people in my office, and I am always surprised at how long it takes many people to answer my question about whether or not they have it. Perhaps it is that they haven't thought much about hope.

Many people respond to the question about hope as if they aren't sure what to say. Those who confidently endorse having hope give me a bolstered assurance that our work together will be beneficial, because people with hope believe all the effort has a purpose. I always fear for those who don't have it.

Even in the worst of circumstances, people can tolerate immense pain if there is hope of change. Unremitting pain without hope of improvement drives people to desperate acts. I see a lot of people in pain. Although hope doesn't take away pain, it is the sense that the pain will improve.

It is important for me to mention here the field of psychoneuroimmunology. Psychoneuroimmunology is at the nexus of thoughts, beliefs, feelings, and the central nervous system and immune function. It is the study of the mind–body connection and how the thoughts and feelings we have affect our body's function.

Over the years, we have found evidence that hope is a key component of psychoneuroimmunology in that it impacts our immune system, the presentation of chronic diseases, neurotransmitters, and more.[13–14]

This next group of stories is about the role of hope in our well-being. It is about finding hope, hanging on to hope, and allowing hope to exist even when it feels like there is no hope.

I think you will find that having hope is reminding yourself that life is ever-changing and accepting that we never really know what is going to happen next. There is such disappointment when we convince ourselves that we know and understand with certainty what will happen next, and there is such freedom in acknowledging that none of us really knows what is around the corner. We have to trust that change is the only certainty. Hope may be that change is coming soon and that it will be the change that we desire. Hope is hanging in there for the next plot twist.

JOURNAL PROMPTS

- What does hope mean to you?
- What have you noticed about your general tendencies around hope?
- Has there been a time when you lost hope? How did you handle that?
- What gives you hope?
- What helps you maintain hope?
- What does hope add to your life?

What Is the Meaning?

. . .

In my experience, hope is dependent on meaning. Meaning is how we make sense of things that have happened or things that are happening in our lives. Within a whole group of people, each might have an entirely different sense of meaning after experiencing one event.

Meaning is actively created based on how we see the world. Our genes may dictate whether we are optimists or pessimists. Our life experiences may dictate if we expect good things for ourselves or not-so-good things. These expectations are the foundation of how we create meaning. Note my use of the word *create*. The meaning we make of events has a strong element of choice, and it all starts with awareness.

While we may be prone to certain expectations in life, when we seek to explain how and why something happens, we are forced to create a story. That story is based on our expectations and how we see the world, but the creation of that story is not so automatic. We have an active role in writing it.

Marty was a fifty-something-year-old guy who had been fairly healthy his whole life. He worked on the assembly line and didn't shy away from hard labor. Now, though, he was feeling the years of manual labor in his bones. Luckily, he had saved well and he could retire early. Marty had big plans for his retirement. He and his wife were going to travel. They planned to buy an RV and see the country.

Marty was sensitive to the privilege of enjoying life while he was able. He had a younger sister who had died of breast cancer just a few years earlier. He had an older brother who was diagnosed with multiple sclerosis ten years earlier, and his brother suffered tremendously until he died the previous year. Marty had been close to his siblings, and he was very involved in helping them through their diseases. Marty blamed his sister's cancer on a history of smoking, and he blamed his brother's multiple sclerosis on bad luck. Marty wasn't worried about his own health because he'd done such a good job taking care of himself. Marty saw health as something a person could control with effort.

One week, Marty noticed severe fatigue that was worsening, he developed a rash, and he had a fever. These persisted. At his wife's insistence, he went to the doctor. One doctor led to another, which led to tests. Eventually, Marty was diagnosed with lupus, an autoimmune disorder affecting multiple organ systems. Marty was devastated by the diagnosis. He was conflicted between feeling that the disease would be a death sentence and the feeling that he could beat it.

Marty sunk into a mini-depression, but as he began treatment, he bounced back with hope. He told himself that while all of this was seriously bad luck, he *could* beat it. He cut out junk food, started eating healthy, and began walking every day. As he started steroid treatment, Marty was frustrated with weight gain, problems sleeping, and irritability, yet he persisted. Then he started having another odd problem.

Marty developed unpredictable, uncontrollable diarrhea. The bowel movements were so unstable that Marty became afraid to go out. He found himself wanting to stick around the house for fear of an episode. All of this led to Marty retiring sooner than he'd expected, but he wasn't enjoying the freedom he'd planned. He had a lot of time, but he felt tied to home. His mood spiraled downward, and he found himself wanting to lie in bed all day. He had no motivation. He had no social life. He'd given up his hobbies. Marty described his life as empty, and he let this go on for the better part of a year before seeking my help.

By the time I saw Marty, his lupus was stable on minimal medication, but he had full-blown major depression. He continued to have significant problems with his bowel function, and there was no effective treatment plan. Marty wasn't sure what I could offer, but he was willing to give anything a try.

Marty told me that he felt punished, but he didn't know what he'd done to deserve any of it. He felt cheated in life. He was angry, and it was all quite understandable. I validated how Marty felt. I got it. How do you make sense of so many bad things happening when you're just trying to do the right things in life?

I explained to Marty that I could not guarantee that working with me would help his debilitating symptoms, but perhaps we could soothe his sympathetic nervous system. I wondered if doing some self-soothing would calm the brain overall and lead to less gastrointestinal reactivity given the strong connection between the brain and gut. We could also just talk about how to manage all of the overwhelming thoughts and feelings.

I taught Marty about cognitive-behavioral psychology, which is recognizing the skewed ways in which we may see the world and learning to argue with unhealthy self-talk. This blew Marty's mind.

Everything we talked about focused on things he could control—his thoughts and his behaviors. The more we talked about what he could do, the more excited he got.

While he knew that he had very real stressors, telling himself every day how bad he had it wasn't helping. Marty was doing a daily review of what he could *not* do, and he was then giving up on the possibilities of what he *could* do. Although it had been there all along, Marty was seeing it for the first time. He also recognized how he was beating himself up for how he was handling it all, and there were cascades of grief, anger, anxiety, resignation, and frustration.

Cognitive-behavioral psychology is not about telling yourself that the way you see a situation is wrong, rather that perhaps your perspective is skewed or biased. It is not arguing with reality or minimizing a tough situation. It is about challenging what you aren't seeing (or aren't seeing clearly) and becoming aware of things you may be saying to yourself that make it worse.

Think of emotions as sometimes being smog that distorts vision.

I asked Marty to do body-scan and relaxation exercises to increase self-awareness. I asked him to practice mindfulness, which, simply put, is to be more aware of the present moment. In being mindful, Marty recognized that he was often living in the future—worried about his next bowel dysfunction or lupus flare. By giving in to his worry, he lost all the potential of the present, and this was a vicious cycle.

Marty discovered that by being more self-aware and focusing on what he could control instead of what he could not, he had more of a life than he thought. Slowly, he began to venture out and do more of what used to make him happy. He could not control his bowel movements, but he could control how he reacted to them. Curiously, they decreased significantly.

Once Marty changed what he was thinking and doing, he began to see his life differently. He began to rediscover happiness. He rediscovered hope for the life he thought he'd lost.

When I asked him how he was able to transcend all the bad things in his life, his response was simple. He told me he realized he had taken much in life for granted. He realized that he actually had a choice. He could choose misery by giving up and waiting to die, or he could choose to make the best of it. While he in no way wanted lupus or bowel dysfunction, Marty acknowledged that he didn't have a choice in that matter. What he owned was what he would do with it all. Marty determined that he hadn't been living a life, and that was his choice. He was now going to choose to hope for something better. He was going to choose to believe that the bad things he'd experienced were meant to help him appreciate every moment he could have feeling good.

In the end, the meaning Marty made of his diseases and life tragedies was not that life was punishing him. If Marty chose to believe that, he had no hope. Instead, he chose to believe that these events could make him stronger. It wasn't that he wanted them. It wasn't that he just slapped positive thinking on the shit sandwich life was serving up. It was that he owned that his choice in the matter was what he would do with it all.

Marty chose hope.

Things happen around us all the time. The sense we make of any events is our meaning. We have biases, but we have ultimate responsibility for choosing the meaning in the end. Meaning affects hope. I've found that people who find something meaningful in tragedy are more easily able to transcend it, but making meaning takes work. It takes reflection and processing.

Researchers who study trauma talk about post-traumatic growth. This is the idea that when trauma happens, as it inflicts harm it also provides the opportunity to experience positive growth as a human being.[14] The growth could be in personal understanding, empathy, patience, and appreciation of life. None of this means that trauma should be appreciated but rather that personal growth can come from trauma with understanding and meaning-making.

Post-traumatic growth involves moving our mindset from the victim of tragedy to survivor of tragedy. The shift in thinking lies within the sense we make of the whole picture. That part is under our control.

I believe that hope lies within anyone's reach. Sometimes it takes more work to find it. In the end, how you see it makes all the difference.

JOURNAL PROMPT

- Think of a time when something bad happened in your life. How were you able to find hope and meaning? How did you move on?

Hope Is How You See It

. . .

I've often heard people share supernatural stories where it seems the dead are contacting loved ones who are still alive. I listen with sincere interest and intrigue, but there is always a part of me that remains slightly skeptical. It's as if I'm afraid of being duped or disappointed. I don't know. Maybe it is the psychologist's mind to doubt.

Then I met Hanna. Hanna consulted me with symptoms of anxiety and depression, but she didn't want medication. She wanted to learn self-help strategies. It was quickly apparent that Hanna struggled with codependence, which I describe as a tendency to spend too much time trying to solve others' problems as if they were your own. People who struggle with codependence feel as if they have no choice but to help and fix, but this feeling is not reality. Hanna was consumed with anxiety, sadness, and concern for others around her, and she did little to take care of herself.

I worked diligently with Hanna on changing that. We even processed some horrific domestic violence that Hanna experienced in earlier relationships. I concluded that Hanna had prolonged PTSD from past abuse, and we worked to find peace and meaning around those experiences.

When COVID-19 hit, Hanna reverted back to being overly concerned with other people's problems. She came to see me following an emergency room visit where her blood pressure was dangerously high. She told me that it was due to stress, and her doctor had changed her antihypertensive medication because the stress wasn't going away. Hanna said that she knew she needed to take care of herself, but she didn't know how to make herself do it.

Uncharacteristically, I raised my voice and said to Hanna that if she ended up in the hospital having had a stroke, she would not be able to help anyone. I went on to suggest that, in fact, by not taking care of herself, she risked making it harder for all the people she loved who would be worried about her and unable to visit her in the hospital because of the pandemic.

Hanna looked taken aback and said she hadn't thought of it that way. She appeared chastened, and I apologized for my tone.

The next week Hanna came back, and she talked about how she was doing a little better at self-care. A coworker had suggested that they virtually make bread together on Saturdays. She went on to discuss what a talented baker her mom was, and the virtual baking reminded her of her mom. Hanna became tearful as she talked of missing her mom, who died ten years ago on Christmas.

Hanna shared about how much fun she used to have with her mom, who was a jokester. Her mom was fun-loving and happy and positive. Hanna told me that she never really got over losing her, and that the pain was so acute the loss felt like it happened yesterday.

Hanna talked about feeling sad that, unlike other people, she hadn't received any signs from her mother. I, again out of nowhere, took a different, lecturing tone of voice and asked Hanna what more of a sign she wanted. Her mother was present in the coworker suggesting that they bake when that reminded her so much of her mom. Her mother was present in things Hanna did that made her think of her mom. Hanna had also shared how she worked to be positive in the lives of others, another reminder of her mother. Once again, Hanna was taken aback. She tearfully said she hadn't seen those signs.

That night I woke up thinking I wanted to share with Hanna an excerpt from Rachel Naomi Remen's book, *My Grandfather's Blessings*, called "Finding New Meaning."[15] It's a story about how we get stuck seeing the world in certain ways and miss so many other things that are going on outside of our bias.

The next morning, I went to get the book, and when I opened it, there was a paper folded in it I didn't remember seeing before. I took it out and laid it on the file cabinet. A few hours later, I finally opened it.

It was a poem called "Death Is Nothing at All," by Henry Scott-Holland.[16] I read it to myself. Boom.

Death Is Nothing at All
by Henry Scott-Holland

Death is nothing at all.

It does not count.

I have only slipped away into the next room.

Nothing has happened.

Everything remains exactly as it was.
I am I, and you are you,
and the old life that we lived so fondly together is untouched, unchanged.
Whatever we were to each other, that we are still.

Call me by the old familiar name.
Speak of me in the easy way which you always used.
Put no difference into your tone.
Wear no forced air of solemnity or sorrow.

Laugh as we always laughed at the little jokes that we enjoyed
    together.
Play, smile, think of me, pray for me.
Let my name be ever the household word that it always was.
Let it be spoken without an effort, without the ghost of a shadow
    upon it.

Life means all that it ever meant.
It is the same as it ever was.
There is absolute and unbroken continuity.
What is this death but a negligible accident?

Why should I be out of mind because I am out of sight?
I am but waiting for you, for an interval,
somewhere very near,
just round the corner.

All is well.
Nothing is hurt; nothing is lost.
One brief moment and all will be as it was before.
How we shall laugh at the trouble of parting when we meet again!

The poem spoke as if Hanna's mother had written directly to Hanna. The poem told the reader that nothing had changed. The dead loved one had merely left the room. Life should go on. The reader should remember the good times and the laughs and not be sad. The poem advised what fun it will be when they are reunited and realize they were so close to one another all along.

I got the shivers, and I put the poem in Hanna's file to share with her at the next visit.

That night, I woke from sleep again, thinking that I should share it with Hanna prior to our next visit. The next morning I called Hanna and texted her a photo of the poem. She called me expressing how overcome she felt. She said, "That's my mother. My mother is talking to me." I responded, "I thought so, too, but I wanted to know what you'd say."

There were too many coincidences. There were the two instances of me taking a maternal tone with Hanna, which was uncharacteristic in our relationship. There were two nights I woke thinking of Hanna and feeling compelled to get the book and look at the poem. The poem, which I'd never seen and which spoke perfectly to Hanna, was in the very spot in the book where I had planned to look.

Losing a loved one can feel hopeless. Sometimes we get so caught up in what isn't there in the form we long for that we miss other signs. I think Hanna's mom was sending her messages, but Hanna was completely missing them because she was too busy missing her mother's physical presence. Her mom had to up her game and get right in her face with it through me. Hanna could no longer ignore the message.

The week after I shared the poem with Hanna, she told

me that on a trip to the grocery store, she found a coffee mug with her mom's name on it. It was an unusual name, and it was the only mug there. Hanna said to me, "I guess my mom isn't done talking to me yet." Hanna bought the mug.

I find hope in the idea that our loved ones live on in our lives even if they aren't there as physical beings. Our job is to allow their presence to be seen, heard, experienced. Hope is keeping the love alive.

JOURNAL PROMPT

- Think a bit about hope and grief. How do they coexist in your life, or do they?

Hope Isn't Mine

. . .

When I was in graduate training, I had the privilege of working on the cancer unit. Perhaps inexplicably, I was excited about the opportunity and eagerly anticipated it. You might wonder how anyone could look forward to working in a unit so full of suffering and death. I can't really explain it other than I've always been drawn to emotionally intense experiences. I think it is because emotions are so authentic and raw.

I recall one patient, Mr. Bedford, who had been given a terminal diagnosis of colon cancer. He was in his midlife and hadn't lived a healthy lifestyle. The diagnosis was a huge wake-up call, and he embraced the opportunity to take better care of himself. He and his family became convinced that he would beat the cancer.

Mr. Bedford wasn't a stupid man. He wasn't delusional. He wasn't hyper-religious, and he wasn't Pollyannaish. Mr. Bedford was an ordinary guy who received the news of terminal cancer in an unusual way. His physicians had been completely honest and provided all of the data to support their diagnosis of terminal colon cancer. Mr. Bedford simply chose to entertain the belief that they might be wrong about the prognosis, and his family supported him.

I was asked to consult with Mr. Bedford, and my approach was to simply listen to his perceptions of the situation. I took my observations back to the interdisciplinary team meeting. Some within the group believed that I should help Mr. Bedford come to terms with reality so that he could make the best use of his time and plan for what he would leave his family. I had never really confronted a situation like this before and had not formed an opinion about the place of survival hope in seemingly hopeless situations.

As the discussion ensued, I began to argue that it was Mr. Bedford's choice to believe whatever he wished. He was cooperative with treatment. He was not behaving in dangerous ways. He was happy. I could not envision a scenario where I would try to wrestle away his happiness. I had no interest in trying to take away his hope, even if I had the ability to do so.

The more I considered the issue and spent time with Mr. Bedford, the more solidly I believed that it was absolutely not my job to force my truth down someone else's throat. I did not have sole ownership of the truth, and the belief that I did would be dangerous. Everyone is entitled to their own reality and as long as they are not behaving in harmful ways, I would not try to take away hope.

To be clear, I am not talking about people who deny truth (particularly scientific truth) for political, financial, or personal gain. That is not hope, and I don't want to conflate these very different situations. Holding on to hope in the face of facts that dispute it because of a belief that things will get better while still doing everything possible to help oneself is not the same as being a truth denier and putting one's head in the sand or using untruths to mislead other people.

I have come to believe that hope for something good or better—even in the face of information that seems to dispute it—serves to improve this very moment, which is all we have. I often preach the gospel of focusing on what we can control: our attitudes. Hope is expecting something better. Why would I ever want to take this from another person if it improves this moment and increases a sense of personal efficacy and control? I cannot envision how that could possibly help.

Hope brings so many benefits. Hope allows us to see possibilities for change. Hope allows us to innovate. Hope gives us energy to hang in there a bit longer. Hope boosts endorphins and mood, and I am convinced that hope may extend life. What I know for certain, though, is that hope makes the time we are alive more tolerable and enjoyable.

Hope improves the human condition.

Without hope, what do we have after all?

JOURNAL PROMPT

- What role does hope play in your daily life? How does hope sustain you in difficult situations? Where does it come from?

Hope for a Good Ending

. . .

Lorraine was a middle-to-late-age lady who came to see me with depression. She was a retired professor, and she presented as very well-put-together. She was polite, well-spoken, and educated. She dressed nicely and was well-coiffed. She had a nice car and good health insurance. She described a pleasant home and family. She wasn't even sure why she was depressed. She just felt depressed.

Lorraine asked me for insight into how she could improve her life. She pulled out a tablet to take notes. She was serious about getting better.

As I got to know Lorraine, it became very clear that her husband was abusive, yet she didn't seem to be aware that he may be a root cause of her depressed mood.

Lorraine's husband had, in the past, hit her and pushed her, but she brushed these occasions off as aberrant and rare. She kept saying these incidents were "in the past."

Despite Lorraine's insistence that her husband was no longer physically abusive, he still violently yelled at her on a daily basis. He called her names like "stupid bitch" and "fucking idiot." Lorraine walked on eggshells thinking that she could keep her husband subdued if she did everything just right. She learned to ignore his name-calling. She said she was "used to it."

Lorraine was surprised when I told her how horrible I thought it would be to live under such circumstances. It reminded me that over time, all of us are capable of becoming numb to horrors in the environment to the point that we don't even realize how fucked up they are.

For many years, Lorraine focused on raising her children and working as an educator. She spent much of her time sheltering her kids from her husband's nasty temper. Now, though, the kids had all moved out. She was no longer working, and he was no longer working. They had no distractions from each other.

Although Lorraine had always told herself that things would be better in the future, that story never quite came true.

The more we talked, the clearer it became that Lorraine felt beaten down by her life, and there was no escape. She was so beaten down that she saw herself as a problem. She felt less than zero. She heard all day long how stupid or lazy she was. She had no positive interactions. She felt she deserved the verbal thrashings. She'd walled herself off from friends. Lorraine felt very alone.

Lorraine had been married to this man for forty-five years.

Without hesitation, I told Lorraine that she'd been brainwashed by her husband, and she was not the problem. The problem was the toxic environment she lived in and the toxic man she lived with. She was dying a slow death from absorbing it day after day. She could no longer differentiate between herself and the poison in her home.

Lorraine appeared shocked at how naturally and genuinely I responded without hesitation. In some ways, I believe she had trouble understanding the depth of what I was saying.

Over the course of several visits, I explained to Lorraine what abuse was. I explained that her husband was physically and verbally abusive. His abuse of power extended to controlling her finances, independence, and freedom.

I could see in Lorraine's face that this was all new information. No one had ever told Lorraine that she was being abused. Because she'd been so private over the years, no one knew to tell her, and no one would have suspected that a person like Lorraine lived with such a monster.

Lorraine expressed pent-up relief as she truly had thought she was rotten to the core, unable to be fixed. What I was telling her was that she was indeed okay. The issue was her husband. We talked about her experience as if seen through the eyes of a child—like in the child development classes she'd taught. If a kid is told over and over that he is worthless, he begins to believe it. Lorraine could connect this idea to her own experience, particularly given that she married so early in life.

At the same time, I knew that Lorraine could not just pick up and leave safely, and I did not tell her to do that. Women have a much greater risk of being killed when they try to leave an abusive relationship. Plus, Lorraine had a lot of important paperwork to get before she left. She had some self-protective tasks to complete. Beyond that, Lorraine needed to process what this new information meant in the grander scheme of her life.

I think Lorraine was grateful that I did not tell her to leave her husband because if she chose to stay, she would feel judged. Instead, I allowed her to process the new perspective I provided, and I trusted her judgment to decide what was best for her own life. As we did this work, I could see Lorraine's mood lift. She started to transcend the abusive experience even though she hadn't left home. She recognized that it was not about her anymore and had never been about her. Lorraine felt hope for something better even though she didn't know what that might be.

I worked with Lorraine for a few months on how to regain control of her life, how to shed the effects of the abuse that had piled up after so many years. I helped her make an escape plan and get the resources she needed to be successful.

Lorraine was ready—but for what? Her symptoms of depression had resolved. She had a plan for her life. She was now pursuing hobbies and reconnecting with old friends. She'd carved out a place of peace.

I was hopeful. Then Lorraine said she wanted to do it on her own. She thanked me for my help, and she stopped coming to see me. I felt so happy for Lorraine. She had gotten a fresh perspective. I worried that she might not leave her husband, but that wasn't a decision for me to make. It had to be her decision. It wasn't mine to force on her as her husband would usually do. I was also sad that I wouldn't be able to see it through—whatever *it* was.

Admittedly, I had some doubt. I wondered if Lorraine would revert back to tolerating abuse and if she was just telling me that she didn't want to change further. At the same time, I had to hold on to hope that Lorraine was capable of protecting herself, whatever form that might take. I had to communicate confidence that Lorraine would do what was best for her in her own time.

What I learned from Lorraine is that we can't judge someone based on the way they look or what they do. She had been genuinely surprised to learn that she was in an abusive relationship. I wondered how one could not know this in today's world, but she didn't. She didn't recognize her experiences as abusive. She functioned just fine, as so many people who are abused do.

Lorraine also reminded me that while I can give information, it is not my job to make decisions for someone else, as if I supremely know what is best for that person. In the end, my role was to label the problem and provide education and support. My job was not to tell Lorraine what to do, and I had to manage my anxiety enough to trust her judgment. The paradox is that if I told Lorraine that I believed in her but undermined her decision-making, I would be another hypocrite in her life.

In the end, I don't know what happened to Lorraine. I am not in the habit of monitoring people without being invited to do so, but I have to feel comfortable knowing that I did what I could. I am okay with that. Sometimes people aren't ready to change in ways that I would prefer. Sometimes they aren't ready to change on my schedule. Sometimes people don't need me like I think they do. Lorraine was a good reminder that life goes on with or without me, and that is completely okay.

What I have is hope. I hope that Lorraine will hear my voice validating her. I hope that she feels empowered to do what she believes is right for her own life. I hope that she finds peace, love, and joy. I hope that our interaction was what she needed.

JOURNAL PROMPT

- In unfinished stories, what is your tendency in filling in the blanks? What role does hope play, and how does that affect your function?

Truth

. . .

I have gone to great lengths to remind you and perhaps myself that I don't have all the answers. To believe that I did would be arrogant and judgmental. I recognize that the story I am going to tell you may sound like a different message. It is not.

Mia consulted me with her husband, Luc. They shared a very tragic story. She and Luc had been married for thirty years and had a daughter, Martine, who was in middle adulthood. Five years earlier, Martine was in a snowmobiling accident, and she sustained a severe traumatic brain injury. Since that time, Mia and Luc had been full-time caregivers for Martine.

Prior to Martine's accident, Mia and Luc had detailed plans for full-time travel when they retired. Both had worked very hard and saved well. They bought a fancy RV and planned to drive around the country—footloose and fancy-free. All those plans changed after Martine's brain injury.

Martine had never married and had no children. She had thoroughly enjoyed the single life, full of adventure and outdoor activities. Her accident occurred on a snowmobiling trip with friends when she hit a tree. She was taken by helicopter to a local hospital, where she stayed for more than a month. It was touch-and-go for a long time and a miracle that she even survived. Mia retired early to provide full-time care for Martine as she had a grueling therapy schedule, including speech, occupational, and physical modalities several times a week interspersed with other medical visits. Treatment had now exceeded five years.

Mia and Luc came to see me asking for my opinion about Martine. Specifically, they wanted to know if I could help her further or tell them how to help her. By this time, Martine had had several neuropsychological consultations to test her brain function. She'd had the best of medical care and available therapies.

They brought all of her records for me to review.

When I saw Martine, she physically moved without problem. But she showed absolutely no sign of emotion. She spoke only when asked questions, and her answers were robotic. Most of the time, she didn't even have answers. She did not demonstrate the cognitive ability to remember information; both her short- and long-term memory were severely impaired. Martine was cooperative, but she clearly appeared to be in her own world. She didn't seem to be troubled, but neither did she appear to be connected to her environment.

Mia told me that Martine was cooperative, but she did not initiate activities on her own. Martine needed instruction to dress and eat and was not psychologically or emotionally engaged. Mia and Luc had insisted on continued therapies over the last five years because they wanted

Martine to have every opportunity to improve. They were compelled to give their all to her recovery. They had not had a vacation. The focus had been singular—get the old Martine back.

Mia and Luc wondered if Martine was depressed. They begged me to tell them what more could be done at this point and wept as they wondered about her level of suffering.

Let me pause here to say that Mia and Luc were incredibly likable. They were earnest and eager. I could tell they loved their daughter more than life itself even though she was a shell of the person she used to be. She was largely non-communicative and seemingly present in body only. My heart went out to both of them.

Mia said that they'd lost all friendships because people stopped coming around. They didn't socialize or leave Martine alone. No one knew how to act around them. Simply put, Mia and Luc were living for the day that Martine would come back to them as her old self.

I asked them what they'd been told about Martine's prognosis. They said that head injuries take a long time to recover from, and professionals had told them that no one could say for sure how improvement would be made. They took that to mean it was still possible for Martine to come back whole to them.

I was overwhelmed with emotion in the moment. I felt only a sliver of the anguish and grief that Mia and Luc felt. I was angry that professionals were not being more direct with them about what to expect. At the same time, I understood that no one wanted to take away their hope of a full recovery.

I decided to give Mia and Luc my brutally honest opinion, and I couched it as that—my opinion. After all, that is what they wanted. They did not need another person to be nice and say what they wanted to hear. Being honest might dampen their hope, but I saw it as data they could use to make future decisions.

I told Mia and Luc that I did not believe that Martine would make further progress. I told them that yes, head injuries do take time, and we can see mild improvements over time; however, five years was long enough to determine her new normal. I told them that I did not think that additional cognitive therapies were benefiting Martine beyond giving her something to do. I also told them that I could not know for certain if Martine was depressed, but I didn't see any sign of that based on their report or my observations. (In folks who are non-verbal, we tend to determine the presence of depression by behavior.) I believed her brain damage was permanent and stable.

I told Mia and Luc that my main concern was caregiver burnout. I told them that it was okay to re-examine their life to make sure their needs were being met instead of feeling like a servant to Martine's therapy schedule. They were clearly shaken by this information and did not schedule another appointment.

A week later, Mia called to see if she and I might meet again. When we did, she told me that she took my opinion right to Martine's treatment team. The treating physician told her that he concurred with my opinion. Mia was floored and more than a little pissed.

She came to thank me for being honest. She was struggling to make sense of how much time, money, and energy they'd been investing in a hope that had been based on inadequate information. Martine's rehabilitation team didn't want to crush Mia and Luc's hope, so the team was not clear about the data.

Mia and Luc were now trying to decide what to do next. They wondered if they should stop therapies. They wondered if they should start traveling with Martine instead of waiting until Martine got better. Mia and Luc were lost.

While I could not provide hard-and-fast answers, I shared with Mia (and asked her to share with Luc in absentia) my bias, which is living today with what we have today. If they wanted to travel, they should travel. They should do what made them happy and allowed them to no longer play servant to a schedule that controls life without realism. I told Mia and Luc to stop looking into Martine's eyes for a sign of her emotional content or discontent, or for a remnant of her previous self. I told Mia and Luc to give themselves freedom and permission to live.

I cannot predict the future, but I can have an honest discussion about the present. We have to make decisions based on the information we have, not what we want or hope for it to be.

I also offered Mia grief counseling. While she was coming to terms with new data, she would be forced to confront some painful realities. Her daughter would not be returning in the form she'd been seeking, and life was forever changed.

Mia came for one more visit, and I sat with her in the pain. It was going to take a while for everything to sink in.

Mia phoned me a few times over the course of the next year. She wanted to provide me updates. She told me that she'd canceled therapies and started planning travel.

Although she was still sad about the loss of Martine's spirit, she celebrated that Martine was still alive. Mia was grateful for the truth so she could live life in the present.

It is interesting that while Martine's professional team had been trying to keep hope alive for Mia and Luc, they were actually creating an unhelpful burden. Mia and Luc felt the need to put off living life to give Martine every chance to get better. If they didn't give Martine their all, they felt unremitting guilt. When they heard a different truth, although it was hurtful, it was a truth that they already knew more deeply. Hearing this truth was freeing. Hearing this truth was empowering. Hearing this truth actually fed hope of something better.

Mia and Luc now had the hope of having adventures with Martine and moving on with life without feeling guilt.

When our original hopes don't come to fruition, hope can evolve. Hope can grow and change. It can be like a weed that just keeps popping up if we allow it. The question is how we see it. Do we see dandelions as weeds or a beautiful pop of yellow signifying life? If your lenses are soiled with guilt and shame, you will only see the distortions. If you only allow hope to take one form—like viewing dandelions as weeds—you will miss the stunning fields of sunshine.

JOURNAL PROMPT

- What is your reaction to this story? I often encounter people who need to play it out before accepting certain realities as truth. Where do you stand on hope in seemingly hopeless situations? When is it okay to move on, and is that giving up hope?

Hope for Happiness

. . .

It's weird that as I get older, life seems to be simpler in some ways and so much more complex in others. Sometimes I overthink and analyze to death things that should be easy. Other things, which I thought were cut and dry, seem much more complex.

Happiness is one of those things that I thought was cut and dry, and now I realize it is anything but simple.

When I want to throw people into an immediate tailspin, I ask, "What makes you happy?" While I am not *that* sadistic, I enjoy having the question in my back pocket for stirring up the conversation. I realize that this question causes a lot of distress because while it is a straightforward question, it can be very difficult to answer.

The first time I asked this question in therapy, I was floored at how powerfully it perturbed the recipient. I tried it again a few times, but each time, I got similar results. It's really kind of disturbing.

Link was a sixty-something, highly accomplished executive who was pondering retirement. He confided that the one thing on his mind lately was how to make retirement a success. This was important because everything else in his life had gone so well. Link found that if he worked hard enough, he could get anything he wanted. He was ready to work on retirement.

I asked Link, "Well, what makes you happy?"

He was initially befuddled and then became visibly agitated. He finally blurted out, "I don't know!" and it was clear that this response was not one with which Link was familiar.

Link worked sixty-plus hours a week. He worked at work. He worked at home. At some point, work took over everything. His kids had grown, and his wife had stayed home to parent them. He didn't socialize much, and in fact, he couldn't name a single friend. His children were also successful, but he didn't feel close to them because he wasn't around much when they were younger. Link had given up hobbies. He had built a nice nest egg, and he had always dreamed of retirement. Now that he was there, he was terrified, with no idea how to be happy or what that even meant.

Delia was a twenty-something who came to see me for anxiety. As we worked through her anxiety, it became clear that Delia was a box checker. Good grades—check. Good education—check. Military service—check. Great job—check. New marriage—check. Delia had done everything right. Since she'd done everything by the book, why couldn't she explain this sense of emptiness, a sense of longing for something more? It quickly became apparent that Delia lived life for others—according to society's checklist of success and that of her partner. Delia had not stopped to ask herself what she alone wanted.

I asked Delia, "What makes you happy?" This set off several weeks of soul-searching and talks with friends and existential angst, but she told me that she was not able to produce any answers. She was bemused by this, but she figured she had youth on her side, which would give her time to figure it out.

Anniah was a fifty-something-year-old woman with two adult children. She consulted me with a sense of sadness and emptiness that she didn't understand. It soon became apparent that Anniah had empty-nest syndrome. She had built her entire existence around her children, and when they left the home, there was nothing left. She'd neglected friendships, hobbies, and interests.

I asked Anniah, "What makes you happy?" and she responded, "I have no idea. I used to know. I loved dancing. I loved volunteering at community events. I enjoyed game nights with friends. But, now, I have no idea."

Such a simple question—a basic question—seems to flummox so many people. And, as you can imagine, if you can't even answer what makes you happy, it would be nearly impossible to decide what to do about it. Determining whether they have truly been happy or if they even know what happiness is typically throws folks into a crisis.

When we are children, happiness just seems to come. We don't even think about it. We go with it. We do what we enjoy. At some point, we naturally have obligations. We have to get jobs, support ourselves, pay bills. Maybe we commit to relationships and have children. Our lives begin to take on identities of their own. We show up and fill the roles without actively considering what we want to do. We do what we *have* to do. We live our lives, but we aren't really present in our lives. We do not live with intention. We live with obligation.

It is easy to see how we get to this place. It is no fun really to consider that happiness takes work. No one wants to think about that. It's so unfair really. We should just "be happy"—another mistaken belief that gets us into trouble.

Everyone wants happiness. Why not?

What not everyone realizes, however, is that happiness takes work. I get that this takes the appeal out of it, but happiness can take a lot of heavy lifting. It doesn't just happen in people's lives. Think of happiness as a return on investment. You have to invest in relationships, hobbies, interests, and life to receive happiness.

The good news is that this makes happiness accessible to anyone who wants it. The bad news is that you have to invest time and energy. Sometimes it is also an experiment because we may not know what makes us happy or we may have forgotten. Sometimes happiness is what we find along the way while we're looking.

I have hope for happiness. I do not believe that happiness is a right in the sense that we must demand it be given to us or sit around waiting for it to be bestowed on us. I believe that happiness is something we can all have if we make a plan and put in the effort. Having hope for happiness makes it all worthwhile. Recognizing that happiness is something that we have to own gives us agency to act upon it, and hope helps us hang in there. If we agree that happiness is not a matter of chance and is independent of material possessions while also being about our own values and decisions, we can have hope that we can design our own definition of happiness and set to the work of bringing it to life.

JOURNAL PROMPT

- What makes you happy? What are you doing—in this moment—to make that happen in your everyday life?

Hope for Change

. . .

D ean was a guy who was crazy in love with his wife. They had a wonderful life together traveling, sporting, and enjoying each other's company. Life was good.

Then Dean was diagnosed with testicular cancer. He was floored. He was healthy and fit. He took great care of himself. How could this happen? Luckily, it was caught early, and he was told that he would make a full recovery with surgery and chemotherapy.

Still, Dean was shaken to his core. This was the first time he'd considered his own mortality, and through this process his body would experience changes to his self-image—particularly his manhood.

Dean dropped into a funk. He wasn't depressed. He was on a journey to acceptance, but he was quieter and more inwardly focused. He had less energy. He was sad.

Dean noticed that his wife wasn't as patient as he'd hoped she would be. She wanted to continue life as it had been. She wanted to have sex as they had. She wanted to be active. Dean told himself that she was just trying to keep up his spirits, but it felt like she was being selfish.

Life was different now. To deny that was to deny his entire experience.

In the middle of treatment, Dean noticed a suspicious text on his wife's phone. After some investigation, he discovered that she was cheating on him. He was absolutely devastated—not just because finding out about infidelity is devastating, but because his wife did this to him when he most needed her.

Dean confronted his wife, and at first, she denied it. Eventually, she admitted that she was unfaithful on a regular basis, but she said it was because she needed sex that he couldn't give her. She made herself to be a victim. She was suffering. She needed to feel wanted. Dean's wife assured him that it was just sex and that he had nothing to worry about.

Needless to say, Dean was worried. He experienced a range of emotions from disbelief to rage to betrayal to heart-wrenching grief. Dean was paralyzed. Luckily, he had a very supportive group of friends and family to lean on, but even that was stressful. They all wanted to protect Dean and encouraged him to walk away from his marriage.

Dean's wife put on a high-pressure campaign to get counseling and repair the marriage.

Dean's confidence was shaken both from the cancer and from learning that his reality was not what he thought it was. He could not make a decision, and so he did nothing.

The thought of leaving his wife brought unimaginable pain, and the lived experience of staying with her, knowing what she had done and was perhaps still doing, was equally devastating.

Dean decided to get professional help and came to therapy. The first visit was fine because Dean simply unloaded all of the horrible details of his illness and discovery of his wife's infidelity. He'd gone over it so many times he didn't even cry. He spoke with continued disbelief and pent-up anger.

The visits after this were much more difficult. Dean expressed utter desperation for answers that no one could give him. Why did this happen? What did it mean for him and for his wife? What was the right thing to do? Where was all of this going?

In the middle of all of these questions, his anguish was overpowering. The roller coaster of emotions—from over-confidence to despair—impaired his ability to function. Dean struggled to hold on to any thread of hope, but he felt he was losing the battle.

To sit with someone who is in this much pain and not jump in to try and fix it is beyond challenging. I wanted to grab him by the shoulders and tell him how to protect himself. I wanted to slap his wife and give her a piece of my mind. I wanted to let my mind wander to other topics so I didn't have to sit and feel Dean's raw emotions.

I did none of these things because that is what friends and family are for—not therapists.

The one thing I could do for Dean was to allow him to feel and be just as he was. I could hold on to hope for him.

I told Dean that I would walk with him on his journey to understanding. I advised him that everything he felt was normal and that he had to feel these things. I promised him that he would not lose his mind. I reminded him he had a right to feel the way he felt. In fact, I told Dean to stop fighting and judging his feelings as he felt them. I en-couraged him to lean into them. The pain was trying to tell him something. I instructed him that if he saw his pain as an emotional cramp, he would see that it would pass. His job was to let the energy pass through him and try to understand the message.

Meanwhile, I told Dean that his only job was to take care of himself with the right food, exercise, enjoyable activities, and friends who would give him space. I strongly recommended journaling to lean into the feelings and help them pass through him.

Dean was skeptical, but he was willing to try anything.

My job was to be patient. I *so* wanted Dean to feel better I found myself struggling to think of some new idea to fix things. I swallowed that feeling and continued to hope that Dean was going to pull out of it. I had hope because I'd seen all of this before. I knew it was normal. Dean had never been in this place before. He didn't know. I had to know for him, and I had to provide the hope, which I did when I told Dean, "Things will get better. I may not know how they will end up, but I know they will improve."

Dean noticed very gradual relief. Of course, it wasn't as fast as anyone would like, but it came. Because Dean allowed the emotions to come and go without judgment or getting caught up in what the emotions meant, he began to see things he had previously pushed aside. He saw his wife's history of selfishness. He saw how one-sided the relationship had become. He saw that he had lost some of his best qualities in sacrifice to her desires. Dean could start to imagine life without her.

Curiously, Dean began to dive into his emotions as a treasure trove of new data. He saw he'd brushed aside many emotional experiences. After about six months, Dean came to a place of transformation. He was brutally honest about how much he'd been lying to himself. He was in no way done with his personal growth, but at least now he felt in control of it. Dean chose himself.

As I think about this story, I am reminded of how much trust plays a role in hope. We trust others to help us find and hold on to hope. We trust that pain eventually passes. We trust that there is a healing process.

In order to have hope in my work, I trust that humans have the capacity to heal, and that capacity to heal comes from within a person, not from me giving an easy fix. The capacity to heal is about feeling accepted, feeling genuinely cared about, and feeling a shared sense of comfort that is the opposite of feeling alone. That is something we can all give to other people, and I feel confident that it makes a difference.

Trust is also about allowing our feelings. This is so incredibly hard when we're talking about pain. It seems to last forever, and it is hard to see where it is going. Digesting pain can feel like we are drowning. We can lose a sense of direction. We can panic. Hope is what gives us stability.

The rub is that we have to feel the pain and trust that it will pass. Think of it as cleaning out a wound. We have to clean out the infection in order to heal. Before we can see clearly, we have to allow the pain. If we try and bypass the pain, we are bypassing proper healing. On the other side of properly healed pain, the world can look entirely different.

When people we love hurt us, that damages trust, but we have the power to allow or disallow the experience to rob us of hope. That is, we have the power to give up hope and trust, and we have the power to hold on to them. No one can take these away unless we allow it.

JOURNAL PROMPT

- Spend some time evaluating your ability to sit with your emotions and listen to your gut. How would you rate yourself on those noticing and listening skills? How does hope color or filter what you notice?

Hope Is the Elephant in the Room

· · ·

Chet was a sixty-something-year-old man admitted to the hospital with horrific abdominal pain. After doctors completed his workup, Chet had a diagnosis of terminal cancer, which had metastasized throughout his body. There were lots of signs that Chet was dying—like a fifty-pound weight loss—but Chet was a warrior. He didn't like doctors or hospitals. He preferred to keep busy and keep his worries to himself.

Chet had been married for thirty-five years. He had two grown daughters and two grandchildren. Chet loved his family, but he was a stoic man of few words. He took the bad news of his diagnosis as you might expect. He showed no emotion. Deep down, Chet felt it was his responsibility as husband and father to show strength. He felt that if he portrayed strength it would be comforting to everyone else. He could not show them that he was afraid and deeply sad, because he didn't want to increase the burden on his family.

Chet's family was a wreck. They fretted and wept outside of Chet's presence, but when they entered his hospital room, they were cheerful. They felt that they had to put on a front of optimism for Chet because he would not be able to tolerate their emotions. They wanted to be strong for him.

I noted during my visits with Chet that he was clearly hungry to talk to someone where he could let down his guard.

When I go into hospital consultations like this, I behave much differently than in the office setting. In hospitals, it is very typical for me to touch someone on the arm in a comforting way, and this is something I rarely do in the office. I find that a simple touch allows people to feel less alone and less like an object to be poked and prodded.

Hospitals render people vulnerable—physically and emotionally. People come in and out of your private space. Patients can't get their own food, go where they want, pee on their own. They are prisoners of a sort—at least in body. The mind is another prison altogether.

I see compassionate touch as counteracting all of the invasive touching.

Hospitals are a foreign land. There is little about the environment that feels healing. They're noisy, public, and unfamiliar. Even information is presented in a strange language. If you're intuitive, it's easy to see that you're not getting all the information. Hospitals have a long, long way to go to be actual places of healing. That is why I touch—to give, not to take away. I touch to communicate that I am there. I touch to convey a sense of peace and connection.

As a way to build rapport, I often ask people in the hospital what lesson they would like to give me to teach others. For Chet, this was an easy question. He said his lesson would be: *Enjoy every moment with your family. Be sure they know you love them.*

We talked a lot about Chet's life experiences, his love for his family, and his wishes around his approaching death. I allowed Chet room to cry, room to fall apart, room to fear. These times can be incredibly painful when you allow yourself to be fully present with someone else's pain. When you are fully present, you don't try to fix it. You don't try to push it away. You try to feel it with them. I often cry too. I sit with them in the pain at that moment.

I wasn't always like this. I used to make big plans about how to help people feel better in the hospital. I realized after trying this, however, that it was ridiculous. People felt bad for a reason, and they had a right to feel bad. My plans for "cheering them up" sent a message that feeling bad wasn't okay.

I learned that by allowing myself to emotionally sit with people in the pain without trying to fix it, they could feel less alone. I learned that was helpful. That was a gift that many others could not give.

It was also hard to see Chet feel isolated from his family and his family from him because of the same disease and the same feelings of guilt, fear, and stoicism.

Because I worked in the hospital, I dropped into patients' rooms randomly. One day when everyone was in the room together, I asked aloud, "What is your biggest fear?" It was a question for everyone. Chet's wife spoke with trepidation. She said, "We're afraid of upsetting Chet. We don't know how to help. We don't know what to do. We don't know what to say." I looked at Chet. His face was quivering.

Other family members chimed in to say that they felt the same. They wanted to talk with Chet but didn't know what to say or how to say it because they didn't want to make it harder for him.

I had to help Chet express himself at this point. I asked, "Chet, I bet you feel the same. You want to make it easier for your family. You are keeping a lot to yourself because you are afraid if you share how you feel, they will feel worse."

Chet had tears streaming down his face, and he nodded.

At this point, everyone started crying and hugging. I told them that so often in situations like this everyone is suffering in silence, but their fears are the same. There is something about saying it all aloud that creates connection. Giving the fears a voice seems to take away their power.

I quietly slipped out of the room.

I visited Chet the next day, and he said that moment was a watershed moment. It led to "a lot of things being said that needed to be said for a long time." Chet was able to express his wishes for how he wanted to die. His family was able to express pent-up gratitude and sadness. They were able to begin the goodbye process.

Chet was discharged home with hospice.

I can honestly say that I have never had anyone react badly when I start conversations like that around death. It isn't easy. The point is that no matter where we are in life, we just want to feel less alone. When we hold back our feelings, we are isolated, lonely, solitary. It is a horrible place to be, and it isn't necessary.

Sometimes, we're so busy trying to protect others that we create unnecessary barriers. You see, we all share universal emotions. To think that we can somehow *protect* someone from their emotions is folly and wasted time. The protection gets in the way of authentic connection.

I think there are times we worry about speaking our truth in fear that it may trod on someone else's hope. At the same time, however, when we don't allow authentic communication, it can take away the hope of connection. It can take away the hope of planning for the future and having a sense of control. Hope is not about some fantasy about the future. Sometimes hope is about relief, and relief involves honesty. We cannot have honesty without authentic communication.

The real task in situations like Chet's is to recognize when we are projecting our own ideas onto someone else. Remember that hope is individually defined, and we cannot possibly manage to understand someone else's idea of hope if we cannot even have an honest conversation around it.

JOURNAL PROMPT

- How are you at difficult conversations? What are you most afraid of when thinking about having difficult conversations with people you love?

Hope Exists in the Dark

• • •

This story is last because I found myself not wanting to tell it because it is difficult to tell, and I worry about being judged. That is why I absolutely need to tell it. I do not include it because the person inspired me. I include it because the lesson is important, and I want to be in the arena of vulnerability.

Mel scheduled an appointment to see me because he wanted to discuss "life stress." His health conditions would not allow him to work or drive; he had almost no social life; and he had very little income. So, yes, that would be stressful.

As is customary for a first visit, I took an extended history. Think of it as a get-to-know-you interview where I get all up in a person's business. In the middle of my intake, Mel told me that he had molested a child in the past. Mel didn't stop there. He spoke as if he were in a confessional telling me about his arrest, prison sentence, and guilt. Mel shared his remorse and took full responsibility. He said he had spent his life since then trying to be a better person. Mel wanted to apologize to the now-grown person, but he knew the apology would be selfish. He would not invade the victim's space again.

The voice in my head screamed, "NOOOOOOO! Stop! I don't want to hear this. I want to leave this room now."

After being forced as a trainee to do therapy with an unrepentant man who repeatedly sexually abused his grandchild many years earlier, I promised myself that I would never, ever put myself in a situation to do therapy with someone who'd perpetrated sexual abuse. It was not something I wanted to do. Had I known this was going to happen, I would not have taken Mel as a patient, but now he was in my office sitting in front of me.

Mel didn't look like a sexual predator (as if they all have a look). He appeared to be an earnest guy, whom I had liked prior to hearing his confession. Because Mel had limited resources and because I had already taken him in, I consciously offered a return visit thinking I would proceed cautiously. I told myself that I would teach some skills without ever having to talk about the sexual abuse again and wrap things up—*fast*.

But that didn't happen.

Mel returned, and it was very clear that his stress was secondary to continued guilt and remorse about the past. As he talked, I was hyper-aware of my curiosity for how sincere he seemed coexisting with my revulsion for what he'd done. I purposefully avoided talking about the abuse, which wasn't the focus of therapy anyway. We focused on acceptance and choice.

All of this was happening while I was weighing whether or not to keep seeing Mel, recognizing that there were few reasonable referral options for him. I was having many internal ethical battles.

The weird thing is that the more I met with Mel, the more I found him to be human and not the monster I initially imagined him to be. I sat through his painful revelation and my own painful emotions associated with listening. Oddly, I found a little bit of hope in that space. When I'd done therapy with a previous sexual predator, that person wanted to blame and deny and seek pity. Mel, on the other hand, did none of these things. He never blamed anyone but himself. He didn't make even one excuse. He acknowledged what he had done was horrific, and he understood the long-term impact his actions would have on another human being.

All of this was very difficult to witness, yet I felt like it needed to happen for both of us.

To be clear, I never thought Mel to be cured of posing a threat. I honestly don't know what that would look like. I would have never felt comfortable allowing Mel to be around children despite the fact that he had many physical limitations. I was surprised, however, at how much time he spent consciously recognizing and managing his past while looking for ways to make amends. Our visits were deeply human. My hope in this case was not in the traditional sense of a person recovering.

I found hope in better understanding the idea of the duality of human beings.

Many people I have worked with are sexual abuse *survivors*, and most were abused by family members. It is not unusual for some of these survivors to tell me that they have conflicting emotions about the abuser. This is a duality of emotion. It is the idea that two opposite emotions about one person or situation can coexist.

There is also a duality of human characteristics. What I mean is that a person can be a terrible human and still have some redeeming qualities. We can appreciate things about a person and find things about the same person to be completely revolting—at the same time. I have seen it over and over. I just had never experienced it at such an intense level as with Mel.

When survivors of abuse tell me about these conflicting and coexisting emotions, they describe feeling *crazy*. That is because they are judging the feelings while simultaneously feeling them. Now, I understood at the gut level. The downside is that folks who experience this duality of emotions around an abuser tell themselves that someone with good qualities could never do such heinous acts. They can doubt and gaslight themselves. I call this self-abuse.

I was able to like parts of Mel and respect what he was doing in terms of how he was now living his life, and yet at the same time, I was completely disgusted by what he'd done. I paid attention to these feelings and could allow myself to feel for Mel without losing touch with the realistic danger he posed.

None of this means that I defend or excuse Mel. I hope to never again work with someone who has molested a child. I have not been transformed. I just have a new experience to consider. This is the lesson.

Around the time I was writing this story, I was also watching *Inventing Anna*[17] on Netflix. This semi-true story is about a real person who fooled so many to the point of their losing significant sums of money. I believe this is a fabulous example of how, despite evidence to the contrary, we want so much to believe the best about people we like that we discount or ignore the red flags. Even the journalist who investigated Anna desperately wanted to believe there was a reasonable explanation for the fraud she executed on others. That's the way it is in life, right? We've all been there. We deny certain realities because we want to see what we want to see.

This tendency gets us in trouble. We do not tolerate the conflicting emotions. We convince ourselves that what we prefer to believe is the reality.

Perhaps because of my psychology background, I understand better than most that even people who perpetrate evil acts have good qualities. Good and bad qualities coexist in everyone to some degree. Mel exemplified this point. No matter how much I liked certain qualities about Mel, I also accepted that he would remain capable of unacceptable violence.

My work with Mel was short-lived, but I learned a very important lesson. When we close our minds off completely, we cannot grow. We lose hope. I had closed my mind because I just didn't want to go to such a dark place, but sometimes we have to go to exceptionally dark places to grow and find hope.

The hope I found is that people can grow—even the ones we despise. (Note: I didn't say change.)

No, I am not a believer that people who molest children can be cured of that attraction, but this story is not about that or even a story about Mel. It is about finding hope in unexpected places if we are willing to go there. It is about accepting that the world is not as black and white as we'd like (even though that makes us feel safer), and all of that is okay as long as there is hope.

JOURNAL PROMPT

- Have you ever found hope in a dark place? How? How do you tolerate or not tolerate conflicting emotions, particularly ones that are highly emotionally charged? How has that worked for you?

Writing More about Your Hope

• • •

Hope can mean many things to many people. For me, hope allows me to tolerate some of the most searing pain that people share. I have had the fortune of seeing people come out on the other side. Because I have seen it enough, I can share the hope with others who have never felt such pain before.

After reading all of the stories about different aspects of hope, what really spoke to you? What things do you hope for in your life? Have you ever been without hope? What gives you hope? What gives you meaning? What gives you inspiration? How can you maximize these factors in your life?

Take a moment to think of your own filters or biases and how these relate to your ability to experience hope. How have your eyes been opened to the presence of hope in your life that perhaps you've been missing?

One of the best times to journal is at the end of the day, in order to allow a better night's sleep. One approach is to write about what meaning you want to take from the day. Ask yourself: *How do I want to close this day out? What gives me hope for tomorrow?* These questions underscore the intentionality of creating meaning and therefore creating hope. They highlight personal agency in choosing how we filter the world, events, and ourselves. It is all about choice and ownership and vision.

HEALING

Sometimes I am overwhelmed at the pain and suffering I see on a daily basis. It takes a toll. I recall that a supervisor once told me that he had to stop working with kids when he began to imagine them all in orange jumpsuits. This is an extreme statement, but it underscores just how difficult it is to hear the stories of abuse, pain, and misery. All of it messes with your head. And it is a paradox because, as a therapist, I want to be emotionally available, but there is a cost.

Hearing and being present when other people are laying out their most intimate pain is an extraordinary privilege, but it is also exhausting because no matter how hard I work to stay separate, the human part of me aches. That is the way it should be in my line of work.

While it may be convenient to be unaffected by people pouring out emotions, I can't do it. That doesn't mean I become so invested that I'm unable to provide a reasonably objective opinion. I just haven't found a way to shut off my emotions. Why would I want to?

Paradoxically, I believe that the ability to ache for someone else and with someone else is healing. It took me a long time to understand this. Therapists are trained to have boundaries, to be separate, to be objective, and those are very important—indeed, essential—qualities of therapy. At the same time, however, they are merely guides for true healers. Being entirely objective is not possible, particularly if you have values and are hearing one side of a story. And if I'm entirely separate, I may not be able to connect in ways that are healing.

The challenges I speak about are not unique to psychotherapists. They are present for all helping professionals. The problem, as I see it, is that other helping professionals get very little training in how to protect themselves from the trappings of giving too much and burning out.

I'm not lying when I say that I have loved people I work with. This may surprise you. In the history of psychology, we have been taught to be clinical and objective—unattached. I get the point of that credo and respect it, but I also think it's bullshit. I'm not capable of being inhuman, and to behave as if I am would be disingenuous. This idea undermines all the work I do.

When I went into the counseling profession, I wanted to save people because, in my ignorant youth, I thought I had the power to do so. This kind of thinking also assumed that people came to me to be saved.

It seems kind of ridiculous now, but it took a lot of work to understand that healing isn't something I'm able to bestow on others by giving answers. If answers were that easy to find, the person seeking them wouldn't be searching.

Beneath all this grandiose and naïve thinking is the notion that people are weak and unable to heal themselves. Of course, when you are the one thinking you just want to *help* people, you don't see it that way, but I'm telling you that it makes all the difference in how you see others.

You may wonder why I'm saying all of this. Maybe you aren't a therapist or someone in a helping profession. Well, I tend to believe that most humans have a drive to help others. When that drive takes over, it becomes unhealthy for our relationships.

This section is for all the humans out there who, by their very nature, want to make life easier for others. It is for all the people who want to help or fix. This section is about changing our ideas of how to be a healing presence in the lives of others.

Let me give you a few things to consider when you think about helping others:

1. Being truly helpful is more about providing a space or vibe that allows others room to figure things out without judgment. When we believe we know what is better, that's really just imposing our judgment. It's the opposite of healing. Healing is accommodating with a calm presence whatever comes to the surface.

2. The power to help also comes with an equally powerful ability to hurt. The desire to help can blind us all to the things we don't want to see or accept, and an unrestrained drive to help can be harmfully one-dimensional and judgmental. Just because you have the power to do something doesn't mean that you should do it. Life isn't *that* easy.

3. Those of us who feel a strong desire to help need to be aware that the desire can make everything appear to be in need of help. We may be prone to seeing things as broken rather than different or adaptable or inherently strong enough to survive. We may be prone to seeing others as victims rather than survivors. When we see the world through this lens, it means we see others and their situations in need of fixing. This can

lead to a feeling of being powerful or valuable. In the end, there is much in the world we cannot fix. This truth can be frustrating and demoralizing. This idea that we can fix needs fixing. Perhaps, instead, we need to focus on healing where we are able.

4. Fixing is not healing. Fixing is trying to impose a solution on a problem, either to try and make another person feel better or make ourselves feel better that an issue is solved. Healing is engaging in a process of making something or someone whole again. It is multi-dimensional, and it is a journey. Healing is about compassion, kindness, kind words, and kind actions. It is about being supportive and considerate, understanding that some problems have no solution. It is about accompanying others on their personal journeys of self-discovery without feeling that we have all the answers for another person. It is about brainstorming solutions when asked and empowering others to choose what works best for them.

5. When you are a helper or a fixer by nature, healing will feel inadequate, but remember that your feelings are not rational. Your feelings come from past programming that doesn't tell you the truth. Feelings are informative but not always accurate. To be a healer involves tolerating the feeling of being inadequate and trusting that the feeling is wrong.

As you read this section, try to remind yourself that helping should be more about healing, as it really isn't in our power to fix after all.

JOURNAL PROMPTS

- How high is your anxiety after reading that intro?
- As you begin to think about your tendency to fix, what are your triggers?
- What has been your experience with helping too much?
- What from your past stands out as a formative experience?
- How has the drive to help caused problems in your life?
- How does helping connect to your feeling important even though it's exhausting?

Unrestrained Drive to Help

. . .

I had to learn the hard way that the unrestrained drive to help others is dangerous. I didn't listen when my supervisor tried to tell me nicely that I didn't have all the answers I thought I had. It had to hurt a little for me to really get it.

This is often how it is in life. A little pain makes the lessons stick just a little better.

I call my early drive to help "unrestrained" because it lacked deeper reflection. When you tell that to young people, the response is often bemusement. An unrestrained drive to help is having a strong desire to help or fix others, seeing problems with others, and commencing with imposing solutions onto others without questioning whether or not you *should* do any of it.

People who are high on the unrestrained drive to help often go into helping professions like counseling, nursing, or teaching.

I'd always known that I wanted to work in a health-care setting with people who have acute and chronic diseases. I was interested in the mind–body connection, adjustment to disease, and immune system function. One of my early assignments was working in an inpatient physical rehabilitation hospital. People were admitted after treatment for strokes, heart attacks and heart surgeries, orthopedic injuries and surgeries, head and spinal cord injuries, cancer, and general debilitation, among other problems. My plan was to spend time getting to know patients and their experiences of illness while helping them cope with illness.

I was young and cheerful. I was also clueless.

Three patients stand out from the year that I worked at this hospital. As I write about these folks, I feel authentically drawn to use titles like Mr. and Ms. because I was a student when I saw them, and I used formal titles.

Mr. Jones was admitted following a liver transplant, and the staff was in an uproar because Mr. Jones said he was thinking about suicide. How could someone who was given a precious resource—a liver—want to die? How could physicians have given a liver to someone who clearly didn't appreciate it?

I don't recall what I was told, but I heard that my job was to go in and fix it. I accepted the assignment with the certainty that I could help.

I smiled as I entered Mr. Jones's room, and he turned to me and asked what in the hell I wanted. I told him who I was and my purpose, and he immediately proceeded to yell profanities aimed at getting me to leave.

WTF?! I was stunned. Could he not see that I was there to help? Why was this man, who clearly needed me so badly, treating me this way?

I dug deep. I told myself that this man was in pain. He didn't know how nice I was. I just needed to convince him of my goodness and my ability to help—no matter what he was dealing with.

I endured several more minutes of angry profanities before finally tearing up. I didn't leave though. Goddammit, I was there to help, and I wasn't leaving until I'd done some helping.

Mr. Jones must have felt sorry for me as he saw my eyes welling up because he softened a bit. He engaged in conversation with me and agreed to let me come back another time.

I did come back to see Mr. Jones each time I was in the hospital, and I came to know that before he was admitted, Mr. Jones drank alcohol heavily every day, which had caused his liver disease. One day, he became very sick and lost consciousness. When he awoke, he'd discovered he had been given a new liver, but he did not recall giving consent for the procedure. He was filled with self-loathing as he felt he didn't deserve the liver. He didn't feel he deserved to live.

Mr. Jones wanted to die as they *should* have let him.

The nastiness he'd expressed to me was, in part, because he was angry and hated himself. It was also a way of keeping those who wanted to help at bay because he believed he didn't deserve it. Helping wasn't working for him at that time.

I saw Mr. Jones throughout his hospitalization, which was lengthy, and I came to love him as another flawed human just trying to navigate the mysteries of life. Mr. Jones was beginning a journey of acceptance that he was alive with a new liver regardless of whether he thought it was just or not. He was also choosing a journey of sobriety at the same time, which necessarily involved reconciling with seemingly unforgivable things he'd said and done.

Mr. Jones was discharged home, and I didn't get to see how the journey progressed. I can only tell you that we began it together with acceptance of what was. One of the greatest gifts of the work I do is that I often find myself beginning my own parallel journey alongside those I serve. I began my journey of self-understanding right alongside Mr. Jones.

When I met Mr. Jones, I believed that helping him meant *fixing* him. I began to understand that helping cannot be fixing. Fixing is not within my power. Even if I could fix one set of problems, a whole new set would pop up.

I didn't yet understand that what Mr. Jones needed was healing—a witnessing or sharing of an experience that no one else was willing or able to do at that point. Healing was walking with him and being with him and accepting alongside him. This is when I began my journey to understanding that true helping is really about being a healing presence.

Okay, on to the next patient. Same hospital. Ms. Smith was in her eighties, and I was asked to see her because she was confused. She was yelling all night and disturbing other patients. The staff just wanted her to be quiet.

When I showed up on the unit, I could hear her moaning aloud.

I went in to see Ms. Smith, and it was soon obvious that she was profoundly hearing-impaired. I told my supervisor that I could not evaluate her mental status if she was not able to hear. He gave me a pocket talker, which is a small box with a microphone that I spoke into. There was a wire that came from the box, and at the end of the wire was a speaker that fit into a person's ear.

I took the device into Ms. Smith's room, and I put the speaker into her ear. I spoke into the box, and she stopped moaning. She looked at me and listened. She answered all of my questions appropriately, and I concluded that she was not confused. She was alert, but she was sensory impaired. She was yelling and moaning because she was profoundly deaf. I informed the staff.

The next time I was in the hospital, I read her chart and saw that a psychiatrist had been called in to see her and placed her on multiple anti-psychotic medications for dementia. This is called *chemical restraint*— medicating a person until the person is no longer a bother. When I used the pocket talker, Ms. Smith told me that she couldn't understand anything the psychiatrist said because he had a thick accent that, combined with her hearing impairment, made the conversation unintelligible.

What I understood was that the staff was tired of hearing her moan, and they needed justification for chemical restraints. While I absolutely understand the annoyance of having a patient moan all the time, I was upset that they had not tried more reasonable measures first.

But more reasonable measures would have meant more resources and more effort.

I was livid. In my self-righteous anger, I saw the staff as diagnosing Ms. Smith with dementia and giving her medication to silence her rather than treating what ailed her. In my view, this was another situation where someone who was elderly and unable to self-advocate was being victimized. I'd already witnessed many other situations where people had been given food but not their false teeth to eat with and where people didn't have access to their glasses to see. This was the last straw.

I ranted and raved to anyone who would listen, and I was zealous in my ranting. Perhaps I had the right to be angry for people I saw being given shoddy care, but my youthful arrogance and drive to fix did not help me achieve the result I wanted. In the end, I was not able to reverse the medical plan. I was a psychology student who was a guest in a medical system that did not care about human beings. The system cared about status quo, compliance, and restraint.

Was I wrong in my reaction? I don't think so. But I was wrong in how I went about it. Although I will never know for certain, others might have been more willing to hear my concerns if I hadn't been so judgmental, so emotional, and so sure that I knew better than everyone else. When the desire to help is so out of control that it drives people to act emotionally, it undermines the whole underlying intention. People were more focused on how out of control I acted rather than the truth of what I was saying. It's much easier to dismiss someone who appears out of control.

Finally, I want to tell you about one more patient, Mr. Roth. I was asked to see Mr. Roth because of depression. I was told that he had cancer, and in the middle of treatment for the cancer, he suffered a stroke. When I went to see Mr. Roth, he had a tracheostomy, and he could not speak. He was able to communicate with me by writing short notes, which was amazing since the stroke had caused some hemiparesis, a weakening on one side of his body.

I learned that Mr. Roth was a retired farmer who had been working as a clown in retirement. I cannot ignore the irony of doing therapy with a former clown who cried each and every time we met. The man I saw was a far throw from being a jester for others' entertainment. He was also far from being a strapping farmer. Mr. Roth was a stricken, physically weak man who could not speak or move well. He didn't even feel enthusiastic about living.

I staffed Mr. Roth's history with my supervisor, who told me that I needed to do cognitive-behavioral therapy (CBT) with Mr. Roth. This meant I was tasked with identifying his pessimistic thoughts and countering them with alternative ways of thinking.

Shit. How the hell was I supposed to counter the thought that life really sucked at that moment for Mr. Roth? By this point, I understood that my original definition of helping (meaning fixing) was fucked up. I understood that helping was about healing, and I decided that CBT was ridiculous. There was no way I was going to argue negative thinking with a man who had every reason to feel defeated and to be angry, hurt, fearful, and overwhelmed.

My supervisor told me that I was taking on Mr. Roth's feelings of despair as my own. I was enmeshed. Hmm. This was seriously problematic because how was I supposed to *not* feel sad about this guy's situation? His prognosis wasn't good. That didn't mean I didn't have hope for him feeling better, but there was no way I was going to tell him he was seeing it all too negatively. I have standards.

Instead, I sat with Mr. Roth. I held his hand. I didn't look away from the anguish in his face as others probably did. I didn't minimize how he felt. I didn't pump him up with cheerful thoughts about how things could turn around and be wonderful and great. Instead, I provided an environment where Mr. Roth could be validated and accepted. I helped him explore possibilities within the new normal, but I didn't try to convince him that he was somehow being a pessimist.

Sometimes being a cheerleader for positivity just makes people feel worse. The unrestrained drive to help can be invalidating to people and rob them of their own journey of growth. This isn't what helping is about.

When I embarked upon my training in therapy, I was not prepared for any of this, and I had no clue that I was an unrestrained helper.

Working with really sick people helped me understand that helping others is really about respecting where people are. It is about understanding someone's experience first, without the judgment or thinking that I know better or could simply fix it all. I have come to know that healing is a much better goal. Healing is about providing a safe place for people to just be. It is within this space of being that makes it okay to explore possibilities. Nothing is off the table because it isn't about just choosing to see the positives or be an optimist. Healing is about providing the message that someone is okay as-is. It all starts with meeting someone where they are.

To be real, the cost of developing this understanding was significant, which is another incredibly important point to make. The drive to help doesn't go away. It is about what you do with it.

I began to drink heavily to cope with not being able to fix things in the way I thought I should. I lived in the world of black and white, where I either solved others' problems or I failed. I drank to numb the feelings of helplessness and sadness. No big surprise: alcohol didn't help, and I sat with a lot of emotional pain with physical hangover pain.

In the blind pursuit of helping, I lost a sense of control and purpose in my life. It is wise to remind ourselves that there are limits. There are limits to what we can do, how much we can do, and how much we should do. Perhaps that's what we say back to the inner voice that tells us we have to do.

I am one of the lucky ones who found that I was doing something all along, which was to be present when no one else wanted to be. I was not looking away. I was accepting. I was healing—and I didn't even know it.

JOURNAL PROMPT

- Think of a time when you got so wrapped up in fixing or saving the day that you were a little (or a lot) out of control. Write about it. What insights do you now have?

Validation

...

Bettye was an older adult when I met her. She'd witnessed a lethal car crash and developed a fear of leaving the house. The fear was paralyzing, and Bettye was driving her family crazy by refusing to go anywhere. They insisted that she see a therapist.

Bettye described straightforward traumatic anxiety about the crash and associated visual imagery, but this is not what was significant. When I take an initial history, I always ask about previous trauma. When someone is consulting me about a trauma, this history is all the more crucial because traumas build upon one another—meaning they are all related in the brain.

I asked Bettye if she had ever experienced physical, sexual, or emotional abuse. She stated that she had, and she went on to tell me that her mother's boyfriend had gotten drunk and raped her when she was seventeen years old.

My response to this revelation was to pause, look her in the eye, and to say, "How awful. That's terrible. I'm so sorry." Bettye appeared visibly rattled by my empathy, and she blurted out, "You believe me?" I replied, "Of course. Why would I not believe you?" At this point, Bettye wept in a heart-wrenching manner. When she composed herself, she told me her story.

At the time of the rape, Bettye was living with her aunt because she didn't have a stable home environment. She didn't want to tell anyone about the rape, and her mother's boyfriend told her that no one would believe her. Bettye traces her history of anxiety to that trauma, which she kept inside all of these years.

At some point, years later, Bettye sought counseling with a male psychiatrist who told her that she'd made up the event because she secretly wanted to be with her mother's boyfriend. He told her that the rape was a figment of her imagination—a figment that she wished had happened but actually did not. Bettye was mortified. She was also young and impressionable, and she began to believe that the psychiatrist was just trying to help her. He was a professional after all. What he told her must be true.

Bettye buried the rape in her mind, telling herself that she must be a really terrible person to fantasize about her mother's boyfriend that way. She went on with her life and was functional, but she had deep self-doubt and debilitating anxiety at times. She went on to get married and have children. She had counseling off and on over the years, but she never brought up the rape again until she met me.

Bettye was unsure of why she mentioned the rape to me. Something made her want to see what I would say. My response of genuine belief without asking her to prove it was more than she could bear. Bettye had never expected or experienced such validation. In fact, Bettye asked me during the next several visits if I still believed her or if I'd changed my mind. She also asked for me to explain and re-explain why I believed her because she didn't trust her memory of what I'd said before.

Once Bettye wrapped her mind around the fact that the rape did happen and that she wasn't just lusting for her mother's boyfriend—an idea that made her physically ill—Bettye wanted to process why the psychiatrist had told her it wasn't real based on the same story.

I explained to Bettye that Sigmund Freud, the founder of psychoanalysis, treated women who were expressing stress and anxiety in the form of physical symptoms, which he called hysteria. Many of these women also told stories of being sexually abused as children. At one point, Dr. Freud believed the women, and then he changed his mind, hypothesizing that it was sexual fantasy and not real.[18] He determined that the conflict these women felt was causing their physical symptoms. Perhaps Dr. Freud could not bear the idea that so many men abused women and girls. Perhaps he was just fucked in the head. Regardless, he inflicted countless secondary traumas on these women by telling them that it wasn't real and that they were making it up in their heads.

Let that sink in for a moment. A person is sexually assaulted and then told that none of it was real. She is told that it is a fantasy that she wished were real. There is the assault or series of assaults, which is horrific. But on top of that, there is being told by a professional that it is all in your head. And then there is the idea that it is in your head because it is what you wanted to happen. Talk about a mindfuck.

This legacy of blaming the victim and treating women as if they somehow wanted to be sexually abused is a true mindfuck that continues to this day. You can see it in the news when women come forward with allegations of abuse and are immediately put under the microscope to determine their believability.

Who gets to decide believability anyway? It seems as though to be believable, a person would have to have no past whatsoever because everything a person has said or done can be twisted into something it is not.

The vast majority of people who confess being victims of sexual trauma have been victims of sexual trauma. While I recognize that there may be some who make up an accusation for nefarious purposes, this isn't the thing that most people commonly concoct for attention. Just look how they are treated. Why would anyone want that?

And while you may be disposed to believe that this is just a painful part of the history of the mental health profession, I assure you it is not. It is ongoing.

Not long ago, a woman told me that her father sexually molested her as a child, which was now open knowledge in the family. When she shared in therapy with a male therapist that the images of that trauma still bothered her, he told her this: The method for getting rid of the images was to play them out in her mind's eye. She was horrified by this assignment and knew enough not to return to see this therapist.

This is not the only troubling story I've heard.

Let me be clear that most male psychotherapists do not practice in this deviant way, but I cannot help but note that the most horrific stories I hear like this seem to involve male therapists. It is the legacy of both Dr. Freud and other men holding powerfully influential positions with women in ways that exploit, harm, and further abuse them.

Back to Bettye.

I saw Bettye for about eight visits. I am not exaggerating when I tell you that in my view, my validation of Bettye resulted in 90 percent of her healing. I accepted what she said as indisputable truth, and she didn't have to prove anything. This led to a deep trust, which led to her getting back out in the world. Once Bettye stepped out, she didn't stop.

Bettye returned to see me within a few months to tell me that she told her sister what had happened when she was young. (Her mother was long since dead.) Bettye's sister also believed her, and it was healing. Bettye was finally able to put it in the past. It no longer hung over her like a shameful legacy she'd created.

I ran into Bettye several years later, and she didn't mind telling me right there that she was still doing great and was still ever grateful.

I don't think we realize how much power words, ideas, and acceptance have in others' lives in both positive and negative ways. I am reminded how damaging influential people can be, particularly when they are damaged themselves or hold damaging views of people they don't understand. The damage can permeate a person's life, and it is all such a waste. I am also reminded how healing it can be to receive validation, particularly when it is so free to give.

JOURNAL PROMPT

- Think of a time when someone said something to you that became somewhat like a cancer in your head, asphyxiating your growth, or a time when someone tried to do this, but it didn't work. Write about either or both. What stands out? How did this play out?

A Calm Presence

. . .

One of the best pieces of advice I've ever been given was from a clinical supervisor on my fellowship. He had a PhD in marriage and family therapy. While I had some training in family therapy as part of my graduate work, it basically scared me. Family therapy can get extremely messy. In my view, when you get too many people in the room, chaos erupts. It is hard to keep track of the unfolding shitshow and to sort through all of the emotional content. Too quickly, everyone can end up hating the therapist as ringleader.

During my training, I saw a particularly explosive family. The parents were each on their second marriage. The husband had three children from his first marriage. His wife had never been a mother before, and now she was stepmother to three kids—one teenager, one pre-teen, and one elementary-school-age child. When I had the family in the room, the stepmother and the teenage daughter acted more like feuding peers than parent and child. The father kept trying to insert himself, but there was no safe place and no safe side.

I could see the problems, but the family wouldn't stop fighting long enough for me to get anything done. Typically, I would end the visits with extreme frustration because I felt like I was only watching the dysfunction and not fixing it. (There is that word again.)

My supervisor, who was consummately calm and reassuring, said to me, "Jodie, the best and most important thing you can do for this family is to be a calm presence."

Let me be real. My first internal reaction was, "Okay, buddy, you live in la-la land. This family doesn't need a calm presence. They need someone to kick ass." At the same time, I respected this supervisor, and I remembered what I tell many patients: "If what you are doing isn't working, what do you have to lose by doing something different?" I decided to give it a try.

Being a calm presence is not just showing up and watching the melee. It isn't giving in or giving up. It is bringing to the space an aura or energy of calm and peace. It is conveying a sense of *I've got this* even if I don't feel I have anything. That isn't false confidence. It is imparting reassurance that I am not flustered or overwhelmed. That I've seen it all before. That I can sit with all of their chaos, and it's okay.

Again, a big part of my ineffectiveness with this family had to do with the notion of fixing. I in no way possessed the ability to fix this family any more than I had a superpower. What would it be like to fix them anyway? The answer would depend on personal values, which are not objective. Fixing could be helping everyone get along, or fixing could be helping the family break up. Who is to say?

All I knew was that I could provide a healing environment for them to sort it all out. When I got flustered, I only added to the sense of agitation that others felt. It did nothing to help.

Regardless of all the epiphanies this experience provided, the story of this family didn't have a happy ending in the way you might think.

The husband and wife ended up getting a divorce, and that was a good thing given all that would come out. The family situation and the marital situation were not healthy, and it created suffering with no end. That is not to say that divorce is easy. Divorce is merely a different set of problems. I am not here to tell you fairy tales. Some relationships are not meant to be, and a healing environment can allow for things to actually heal.

I think my idea of helping was to stop the fighting. In the end, I think the fighting needed to happen to get to the eventual outcome. I could not fix what was not meant to work.

Helping is not saving. Helping is not fixing according to our own values.

The lesson of being a calm presence in the world has been invaluable to me. Conveying a sense that no matter what people tell me, I can handle it has been the hallmark of my work. It has been the foundation of what I believe has been more healing than anything else I have done. Being a calm presence allows people to unpack much of what they've been carrying while having confidence that I am with them. Being a calm presence is contagious to others who may not experience calm anywhere else in their lives.

I have found that being a calm presence also allows me to save my reactions and process them productively in the appropriate time and place. It is how I have parented my kids, and I believe they feel comfortable telling me many things I don't necessarily want to hear! I take it in as if I expected it all along. My goal is to communicate a feeling of *I've got this, and I will help you get through this.*

I am not shocked. I am not repulsed. I am not going to run away. I am accepting. I am here.

This may be more help than most people have received in a lifetime, and it is something that any of us are capable of doing if we allow it. It starts with managing our own emotions first. Sometimes this can feel monumental, yet it makes all the difference.

JOURNAL PROMPT

- Have you ever been with someone who brought a calm energy? If yes, what is that like to experience? How would your life be different if you were able to be a calm presence, and what does this mean for you personally?

Those Damned Triggers

...

We all have triggers, even me. Those who don't know or understand their triggers are at the mercy of them.

Years ago, when I was in training, I was asked to see a young boy whose good friend was found deceased hanging from his bunk bed. As I type this, I am aware that the boy's first name popped into my head. Memories are so strange. Often, I can't recall details when I want them, yet other times, they slap me in the face out of nowhere.

I'll call the boy Henry. Henry told me what happened and explained that he was not sure if his friend had killed himself on purpose or by accident. Like any good student, I pored over the scientific literature and found that childhood suicide is such a low base-rate event that we didn't know much at the time. Often, however, adults prefer to believe that it is accidental, so we go with that explanation.

My job was to help Henry with grief, but Henry held it all in. He was a tough guy who bought into the "boys don't cry" mentality. No matter how I pushed, I received nothing.

I set up an appointment with Henry's parents to get them on board to help Henry grieve. They didn't want to talk about any of it. They wanted to pretend it would go away. I could see that they didn't encourage Henry to express sadness, but I was on a mission to make it happen.

During supervision with my professor, I bemoaned what terrible parents Henry had. I insisted that Henry needed to cry. My professor politely pointed out my judgmental nature and subtly referenced that I might not understand the complexities of being a parent. I blew that right off.

You see, my plan was to work with kids because I was going to save every last one of them. I had that power. I just had to show everyone else, so I kept pushing.

I met with the parents again—nothing. My supervisor got more in my face, and I won't ever forget his words: "Don't ever take someone apart if you can't put them back together again." Boom.

I realized that Henry was indirectly telling me that it was not safe to grieve. He would not be supported. He didn't have the ability to let go because he might not be able to get it back together. I was asking him to do something he intuitively knew was not going to go well. Who the hell was I to impose my will upon him when he was not ready? How disrespectful was that?

Luckily, I got the message and continued to lend support to Henry while allowing him to follow his own wisdom. I comforted myself by thinking that I offered Henry a different experience relative to emotional expression, but I had to leave it there.

My time with Henry should have been a hint that perhaps I wasn't cut out to work with kids, but I simply refocused to work mostly with adults with occasional pediatric work. Though I had some awareness that my kryptonite was a desire to save children, I thought I could control it.

It was not until I worked with a number of families where the father was abusive and reckless with the safety of the children that I made the call to step away from work with younger children. I had to embrace that I am simply not equipped to resist looking into their doe eyes, when all I see is that they are struggling to understand why I cannot protect them. I am not fortified to manage these interactions in a way that allows me to sleep at night. The final straw was when I got myself into trouble overstepping my bounds in a misguided attempt to protect a child. I made it worse.

Yes, sometimes the message has to get so loud it knocks us down.

Never take someone apart if you can't put them back together. Also, never take apart a child's situation if you can't absolutely ensure that you will put it safely back together. Despite my delusional power trips born out of a desire to fix, I had to face my failings.

When emotions take over, irrationality sets in. Narcissism is in control.

This story is essentially one about boundaries. Any of my close colleague friends will tell you that I am a freak about appropriate therapeutic boundaries. I typically respect the hell out of them. I have learned to sit with others' pain and not try to fix it. The pain is not mine to fix, after all. Plus, when I feel compelled to step in, it gives the message that I see others as weak and unable to solve their own problems. I have learned to tolerate my own anxiety and recognize my limits.

Before I understood this, I acted on the trigger, and every time I have done so, I have experienced incredible regret and remorse. The end result is never what I predicted with my good intentions. Yet, good intentions are not enough. Good intentions like this are based on emotions. In my case, it was an emotional drive to fix and save, yet I am not all-powerful.

It is not unlike putting myself in a room full of decadent desserts and telling myself I will have just one bite. My intention starts out okay, but the end result isn't consistent. It was probably never an honest conversation to begin with.

We all have these kinds of triggers. Perhaps we know this already. Even if we do, do we fully understand the extent to which they can control us? Have we figured out how to identify them before they become a problem? Have we figured out how to tolerate the emotions and not act?

This is especially the case in wanting to fix. Consider your career. I have yet to meet a nurse who wasn't a fixer. The same could be said for therapists, teachers, and ministers. We may even feel called to certain careers that allow us to use certain drives for good. However, the drive to fix gets in the way of others learning to fix on their own. The drive to fix stunts others' growth. That isn't how we tend to see it, though. We see it as not doing enough. We see it as turning our backs.

In the end, we are who we are. You cannot change who you are, nor should you necessarily want to do that. What you can do is be honest with yourself about what you bring to the table. Accept it. Understand how it affects you and drives your behavioral choices. Only then can you begin to control the drive rather than the drive controlling you.

In cases where you want to help or fix, remind yourself that this is a wonderful quality, but fixing doesn't mean rushing in to eliminate the problems. It is being empathetic, supportive, and encouraging of other people to fix their own problems. It is seeing some pain and suffering as necessary to the other person's growth. It is helping other people learn skills.

To be clear, I am not talking about refusing to help save someone's life or give someone food or to intervene in humane ways that protect other human beings. I am talking about situations when we fixers do too much, when we cross the line, when we are triggered.

Bad shit goes down when we think we have the answers to others' problems. What we may end up creating is a whole new set of problems called unintended consequences.

Instead, what if we learned to give others and ourselves the message that:

- You are not so weak that you need me to save you.
- You've got this.
- I am here with you every step of the way.

I'm proposing that you are so much more helpful when you allow yourself to simply be present and witness rather than judge and intervene. I am proposing trust.

JOURNAL PROMPT

- What is your history around boundaries? What are the triggers that erode your boundaries? What is your kryptonite? What do you need to do about it?

Becoming Whole

. . .

I had known Roxanne for years. She first consulted me ten years ago with an anxiety disorder. We'd tackled relationship conflicts, boundaries, self-esteem. Roxanne had admitted that she was a binge drinker, and I advised her many times over the years that she should stop drinking. She thought I was overreacting. I understand that for someone to change, that person has to be ready. My job is not to nag or judge. My job is to be on the journey as they come to new levels of self-understanding.

I had a nice relationship with Roxanne, and she consulted me off and on over the course of time.

Roxanne returned to see me midlife. She felt like something inside her was different, and she wanted to make her life better, although she wasn't entirely sure of the specifics. She described her life as unfulfilling. She didn't like her job. She wasn't happy with friends. She had a tough time putting words to her discontent or what particularly she wanted to change. She just knew her anxiety was out of control.

Roxanne is like many women I know who have a psychological shift in middle age. Somehow, they seem to grasp that life is time-limited and begin to recognize and resist some of the restrictive messages of society. They begin to feel more comfortable in their own skin and more confident in their abilities.

Roxanne took the bull by the horns and made a huge career change to interior design and decorating. She'd always had a knack for it, but she'd second-guessed herself into never exploring her potential. The basic problem had always been that her family needed her income, and she was too afraid of not being able to bring home some bacon. Well, Roxanne was an instant hit and garnered more business than she could manage. She started making more money than her husband. She felt like walking on air—at least where her career was concerned.

Roxanne came in one day stating that she worried she was an alcoholic. One of her friends had admitted that she was, and now Roxanne was questioning herself. Following lengthy discussions, she decided to try alcohol abstinence. She was drinking heavily in the evenings for her "nerves" and to help her sleep. She wanted to see how life would be if she didn't use alcohol anymore. She also decided to attend AA regularly.

Roxanne discovered that her anxiety was much improved off alcohol, but she noticed how restless she was in her life. It was as if she was looking for something, but she didn't know what. She could more clearly articulate what was missing in her marriage and overall life, but she still wasn't sure what to do about it. Meanwhile, she continued with AA and found that working the steps was very enlightening, even if she didn't fully embrace that she had an issue with alcohol.

One day Roxanne admitted that she was consumed with resentments that even she identified as nonsensical. She always knew they were there, and it was becoming harder to ignore them without alcohol. It had been apparent for a long time that Roxanne was very self-judgmental and often relegated herself to lose-lose scenarios in her own mind. As we were discussing this, Roxanne talked about her evangelical upbringing, with its extreme delineation of right and wrong. It seemed that she had learned to sit in judgment of herself at all times. She felt paralyzed at times with fear of doing the wrong thing. She judged her every action as wrong.

I threw a transactional analysis[19] conceptualization by Roxanne. When we are born, our self consists only of the child—the part of us that wants what it wants right then. The child is immature, prone to anger, temper tantrums, and fits of humor. As we have more exposure to parental figures, we develop another aspect of self, consisting of the conscience. This is really the parent. It is the part of us that learns rules, boundaries, morals, right versus wrong, and judgments. As we continue to age and develop a sense of our own identity beyond our parents, we develop our adult selves. This is the part that contains confidence in our own abilities. It is the unique part of our selves that contains the adult balance between the child and parent parts.

The development of the healthy adult self depends on being given opportunities to be independent. It helps if our parents and teachers communicate faith in our ability to make independent decisions. It helps if criticism is constructive and not internalized as a sense of being damaged.

I explained how the parts of our self are supposed to develop. Sometimes things go wrong. For Roxanne, the extreme moral judgment of her upbringing that was omnipresent led to the parent part of her self being overdeveloped. In fact, the parent part of her self became so strong and powerful that it became abusive and domineering to the other parts. Her mother also had anxiety and behaved in a controlling manner out of fear that something bad would happen to Roxanne. Roxanne was not encouraged to do things on her own, to learn self-confidence or self-agency. She was reinforced to always be wondering what God would want her to do and what others would think. She learned to judge herself in the harshest light. Roxanne learned not to trust herself. The child in her learned to remain needy and unheard, and the adult never fully developed because of shame, guilt, fear, and self-doubt. This left the parent to become an abusive bully. Drinking was the only way she'd found to shut the abuser down so that she could rest her mind.

Roxanne lived with this until she reached midlife, and then she began to question everything. Through our work, she took small risks and saw that, indeed, she did have talents, skills, and abilities of which she could be proud. She slowly started to shed the extreme ideas of good versus bad in lieu of a more nuanced view of the world in shades of gray.

The resentments Roxanne felt were not toward other people, really. They were self-resentments for not protecting herself against the abusive, judgmental parent in her head. It seems she never showed up to take her own side. Typically, this is what the adult part of the self is charged with doing. The adult takes all of the emotions and makes sense of them. The adult says it is okay to trust the self.

When Roxanne asked how she could overcome the self-abuse, we talked about it as a process. The first step was recognizing that the abuser lived in her head. The next step would be empowering her adult self to show up and practice making decisions. While it might seem a little adolescent, Roxanne needed to go back and do work that developmentally would have been done when she was a teenager. She needed to re-parent herself.

While Roxanne found understanding all of this to be so validating, it wasn't enough to enable broad-based change. This was a journey. The cool thing was that Roxanne was a good mother. She knew how to provide unconditional love and allow her kids the room to make mistakes that she was never allowed. I reminded Roxanne that she could now give this to herself. She needed to allow herself to make decisions with the freedom to make mistakes—and in fact, they wouldn't even be mistakes, just different choices.

When Roxanne found herself falling back into the deep-seated feelings of shame and guilt, I asked her what she would tell her children. She would intuitively know it would be the opposite of what she was saying to herself. That simple cue would remind her to reset what she was doing to herself. She would often say, "I keep forgetting to do that part."

I can't give you an end to this story because the end only comes at death, and Roxanne is still in the fight. The amazing thing, though, is that once we recognize we have the ability to give to ourselves at any time what we didn't get in childhood, we are ready. It is a moment-by-moment journey of recognizing that we internalize fucked-up messages and ideas and then reminding ourselves at some point that we get to choose which ones to believe.

Healing is a gift we give ourselves with all of the kindness, love, and compassion that we would give to others in need.

JOURNAL PROMPT

- In what ways do you beat up, judge, and shame yourself? Why do you think this is, and how has this affected your healing in difficult times? What do you want to do about it now?

Letting Go of Pain

. . .

I've heard a lot of personal stories that involve tragic circumstances, and despite doing this for more than twenty-five years, I have not become hardened or callous. I am not immune to the suffering of the storyteller.

One story, upon retelling, invariably makes me weep. It is a story that reaches so far into my soul that I feel its gut-wrenching power anew each time I consider it.

Suzanne had a beautiful family. She was married with two young adult children. Her oldest daughter, Michelle, had just started graduate school in nursing. Her youngest daughter, Jacque, was a graduating high school senior. Suzanne had a wildly successful career in corporate sales and eventually worked her way up the executive ladder. She seemed to have it all, and she was very aware of how lucky she was. She chose to spend weekends with family and friends, engaging in a host of outdoor sports and doing community volunteer work as a way of giving to those less fortunate.

Suzanne was not a deeply religious woman. She believed in a higher power, but she didn't attend church regularly. However, she had a strong moral compass and call to serve others. She was very close with both of her children, but she was particularly close with Jacque as her youngest. Jacque had always been exceptionally mature for her age. She was a goofball at times, for sure, but she seemed to have a wisdom that exceeded her years. Jacque was a straight-A student who had a full-ride scholarship for college awaiting her after graduation. Her whole life was ahead of her.

One day, Jacque was the passenger in a car driven by a classmate, whom Suzanne did not know well. They were hanging out after school, and the classmate was texting while driving. The car left the roadway at a high rate of speed, and Jacque was killed instantly in the crash.

Suzanne described the moment she learned of Jacque's death as being devastating and life-altering. She said it felt like time stood still. In fact, Suzanne could barely remember the six months that followed Jacque's death. She sought religious counseling despite feeling like she'd lost her faith. She sought counseling with a spiritual adviser. She sought counseling with a therapist. Suzanne was desperate to find some sort of understanding, insight, healing. She could find nothing to ease her pain.

Suzanne was angry at the world and herself for allowing Jacque the freedom to hang out with someone she didn't know well. Suzanne distanced herself from her family and friends. She became despondent, and her career suffered even though she threw much of herself into work. No matter how much Suzanne sought enlightenment and peace, it eluded her.

Suzanne thought that perhaps prosecuting the young driver of the car would provide some relief, so she fantasized about punishment. She believed if she had more dirt on the driver, it would validate her desire for revenge, and this desire was taking up more and more mental space. Suzanne threw herself into finding justice for Jacque and did a deep-dive online for background on the classmate.

Suzanne discovered that the classmate was also a straight-A student who had never been in trouble. She, too, was headed for college on a scholarship, but her life was entirely different from Jacque's. She came from an economically disadvantaged background. She lived with her single mom, and her dad wasn't involved. The classmate worked as a waitress on weekends to save money for school. Her major was to be education, and she planned to be a teacher. One of the significant factors in the classmate receiving a scholarship was that she had a history of long-term volunteer work within her community. By all accounts, the wreck was caused by an error in judgment—a mistake.

Suzanne felt compelled to meet with the young woman, even though she was not sure why. She was increasingly uncomfortable with plotting revenge. Somehow Suzanne thought it would bring her closer to Jacque's spirit. She was surprised to hear that the young woman was agreeable. A hasty meeting was arranged.

As the introductions were being made, the young woman began to weep in shame, agony, and fear. Suzanne was overcome with sadness and compassion. She walked over to the young woman and hugged her like she wished she could hug Jacque, and they both wept uncontrollably. The young woman repeated "I'm sorry" over and over.

This moment lasted what seemed a lifetime, and Suzanne described it as something heavy departing her body. It wasn't that her grief was taken away. It wasn't that she was no longer sad, but her anger was extinguished. She felt at peace as much as a mother who had lost her daughter was capable at that moment.

Suzanne requested that the prosecutor not pursue harsh punishment. She felt the young woman's guilt and remorse were enough. She wanted the driver to go on with her life and to use the experience to help others. Ruining another life would do nothing to relieve her own suffering around the loss of Jacque. She would get no pleasure and would, in fact, feel worse.

This is what healing looks like.

I would like to tell you that Suzanne was all better. She was not. She simply felt different. She felt good about her decision, but she would never recover from the loss of her daughter. She would always miss Jacque, and she would always feel like part of her was missing. She went on with her life, but she did so knowing that she had given the gift of redemption to another human being.

I would like to tell you that this young woman was transformed from the interaction. I would like to tell you that she used the experience to persuade others to avoid distracted driving. I would like to tell you that she went on to do good in the world, but I don't know. I cannot say.

I can only tell you that the interaction between Suzanne and the young woman who accidentally killed her daughter was healing. I say that not in the sense that it took pain away, but in the sense that two souls met in a lonely, miserable place and shared connection. Two souls met and accepted each other as human.

Suzanne forgave the young woman, and she set herself free. The young woman was able to ask for forgiveness and be granted that. When I tell this story, many people say that they don't know if they could do the same thing. I understand that, which is why the story is so touching. It is a story of people at their best, maybe even superhuman, being able to find peace in the worst of circumstances— being able to let go of anger, resentment, and revenge in exchange for peace and acceptance.

I rarely use the word *forgiveness* because people get too caught up in thinking they are gracing someone with a gift they don't deserve. If we waited to forgive based on the other party's deserving it, no one would ever forgive. Forgiveness is about finding peace for oneself. It is a gift we give ourselves. It is not forgetting. It is a conscious cutting of ties with negative emotions that eat our soul and kill us inside.

If we are honest with ourselves, we can admit that we have all fucked up, and we are all at risk of continuing to fuck up. Hopefully, we have not fucked up in ways that kill another person or ruin another person's life, but we're all capable of that. And though we might tell ourselves that revenge or anger will somehow provide comfort, it does not.

Healing is being vulnerable, being honest, being human with one another. Healing recognizes it will never be enough and it is always enough at the same time, and healing is accepting that reality.

JOURNAL PROMPT

- What hurts are you holding on to from the past, or what hurts have you let go? Why? How has your choice to hang on or let go affected you?

People Just Want to Feel Less Alone

• • •

As a kid, I didn't watch *Mr. Rogers' Neighborhood*. I thought it was too lame and cheesy, but I found myself wondering about the movie *A Beautiful Day in the Neighborhood*[20] when it came out. I'd heard good reviews, and I thought it would be something healthy to do with the kids. I was not at all prepared for the gut punch in this movie.

As I watched the movie, I became increasingly stirred emotionally. I was looking around to see if anyone was looking at me because I could feel an emotional tidal wave. Before I knew it, I was crying—a little uncontrollably. I looked over at my teen boys, wondering if they had noticed my tearfulness, but they were completely engrossed in the film. They never noticed me at all.

The message of the movie was so simple, so exquisite: All people really want is to feel less alone. Feeling heard, understood, and validated, and, most importantly, feeling connected leads to healing.

So, I should know all of this, right? I did. Sort of. The movie reminded me of how very important acceptance is to healing. I think all of us sometimes get so caught up in doing and moving and fixing that we lose sight of being and accepting.

As I've mentioned, people are prone to falling into a big trap called "I can help fix that." If we're not aware, we can fall in and have a hard time getting out. Helping becomes all about problem-solving and less about healing and being with another person who is in pain.

I believe that it is being with—truly with—the person that allows deeper-level healing.

Research on the outcomes of therapy clearly show that it doesn't matter what type of therapy one receives, the gender of the therapist, length of practice, and more. What predicts therapy outcomes is the connection between the therapist and the patient.[21]

This connection is what heals. Why?

Deep down, we all have that sense of being alone. Negative beliefs about self—like *I'm not good enough*, or *I'm not lovable*, or *If people really know me, they will think I'm fucked up*—can worsen that feeling of aloneness. Even without these negative beliefs, we all know that no one can truly share our pain at the level we feel it.

These feelings can easily lead to a sense of complete aloneness, isolation. That is a very scary and lonely place. It is a place where we ruminate on all of our flaws under a microscope. The sense of shame and guilt can be searing.

Being in the presence of someone who calmly accepts all of that and is still able to convey that acceptance along with respect, care, and compassion is the balm of healing. It is not feeling so self-assured that you have the answer to another's problem that you should jump in and fix it. Because the problem isn't really the problem. The problem is how the person feels in that moment that is skewing everything else.

Mr. Rogers seemed naturally able to do all of that. You may call this *super empathy*. Perhaps that's right, but it is also a willingness to be there in the dark place where it can sometimes feel like one will drown that true healing takes place.

To be with someone in a dark place without feeling the need to lecture, judge, or fix is a true gift we can give to those around us and even to ourselves. I call this being a healing presence, just like Mr. Rogers. You can help people name the feelings and validate and normalize the feelings without ever trying to argue, minimize, or talk someone out of the feelings.

A healing presence accepts. Stop for a moment to think just how powerful that message is in the lives of children, who are so often told, *No. Stop. You can't. You shouldn't.* Think of it as soil. If you plant a seed in really good soil, it has a much greater chance of growing into everything it is meant to be. When you plant the seed in questionable soil or don't water it or fertilize it, it may not grow as well, as strong, or at all.

Mr. Rogers's story is about connection, and though it is very simple, it is also very difficult to accomplish. Connection is about being emotionally available to others and accepting of what they need to share. Sometimes the things that people share are real downers. The stories may be disgusting, heartbreaking, or miserable. They may also be uplifting, inspiring, and exciting. Connection is about being open to all of it without trying to change, argue, or dismiss. It is about having the comfort and confidence to allow what is said to be said. It is about creating an environment that validates our humanity. The hard work of deciding what to do about it comes later.

JOURNAL PROMPT

- What relationships do you have where you feel safe, connected, and accepted as you are? How do they contribute to your healing?

All the Difference

. . .

When I was twenty-one years old, I began entertaining the idea of going back to college. I had a two-year medical transcription degree and worked low-wage jobs in the medical field, but I longed for something more. I enrolled in night classes at the local community college, but I was only semi-serious. I was drinking and partying with friends. I wasn't showing much real promise.

Even so, school was easy for me, and I liked it as long as it didn't interfere excessively with my good times.

One night after a test in a composition course, I was on my way out the door when the professor asked to speak with me in the hall.

I said, "Sure."

I don't recall the exact conversation, but I clearly recall the message. Judith, my professor, asked me if there was a reason I wasn't applying myself. She was under the impression that I had a much higher ability than I was demonstrating in class. She asked if there was something getting in my way. Busted.

Judith was very politely calling out my bullshit. What Judith was saying in actuality was that she could see me. She could see *me*—the real me. Judith could see someone throwing away an education. She could see someone with intelligence and potential. She could see someone with worth and depth. Judith could see someone who didn't seem to care but actually did care. Despite what I'd been telling myself, I was not invisible.

This was a turning point for me. Judith was a respected writer for the local paper. She was a quiet intellectual who kept to herself. If Judith cared enough to pull me aside, maybe I should listen.

After this crucial conversation, I got more serious. I applied myself and tried to gobble up all that I could. I made commitments to transfer to a university and began to entertain what I wanted to do with my life beyond having a good time.

I had good teachers as I was growing up, and I also had friends and family who cared about me. In fact, I had no good reason to blame for the way I was throwing away my potential. In retrospect, I don't know that I perceived all opportunities as being open to me. Although I had a great childhood, we were, in fact, low-income by today's standards. I had no college fund. No one in my family had been to college. It sounded good, so I thought I would take some classes, but I had no idea it could go anywhere. No one had ever told me that I was college material. Honestly, I think Judith was the first person to suggest that I was.

Let me take it further. I believe I was routed on the non-college path in school because of lack of means. I came to believe I should set my sights on a good husband and kids as the primary goal in my life. To be clear, there was nothing wrong with this as a goal, but not as the only goal I could set for myself. I did not consider any other paths as applicable to *my* life. A major problem with the goal of finding a mate was that I wasn't any good at it. I didn't date much. I was also easily bored due to excessive curiosity.

I loved school, but I knew enough not to act smart because smart girls weren't very attractive. I wanted to be fun. My senior year in high school, a good friend was enrolling in a transcription program, and it seemed affordable and interesting. I jumped on that bandwagon. I could learn something new and still have plenty of time for fun.

All of this makes me realize how important high school counselors are in influencing the choices of adolescents. If a counselor doesn't see college potential in you for whatever reason, you are not encouraged to pursue college. Without encouragement from an adult in the know, how else would an adolescent know about multiple feasible paths? My family didn't possess this expertise.

I am not saying that a college path is superior or even right for everyone. Rather, my point is that all options should be perceived as being on the menu.

I keep thinking that Judith could have easily passed me along. She could have saved her time and energy. She could have seen me as another burnout not worth the effort, but Judith saw past all that. She took a risk and confronted me. What risk did she take? Well, I could have gotten upset. I could have been another disappointment. She confronted me anyway.

All my life, I'd been average in my mind. I'd been invisible in public. I was smart, but I wasn't the smartest.

I downplayed what I did have in order to be more fun. I wasn't athletic. I wasn't a born leader. I wasn't a cheerleader or popular. I was average in every way. There is nothing wrong with average, but to me, it felt like *nothing special*. I felt invisible. I wanted more, but I didn't know what that could be. I was never able to find the courage to believe I deserved more, was capable of more, or had the option of more. What if I failed? What if I couldn't do it? I had supportive family for sure, but they had to be. Judith, on the other hand, was a person who of her own volition sought me out to say that I had promise.

What I didn't know at that time was that I had generalized anxiety disorder. Generalized anxiety disorder is what I call a worry disorder. It is a disorder that causes intense self-doubt and excessive and uncontrollable worry about everything. It is difficult to manage, particularly if you don't know you have it. I never told anyone about my anxiety. I didn't even know that it wasn't normal. All I knew was that I could fit in if I was drinking, so I partied a lot. I'd finally found where I fit in, but the direction wasn't good.

Judith saw through all of it. Teachers do this. Every. Single. Day.

What is important about this story?

As we go through life, it is easy to become oblivious to the impact we have on others around us. It is easy to look the other way. It is easy to say that it is not our responsibility. We can also be hardened to the profound influence we may have on others around us. I suspect this is because we don't see the immediate results of our interventions.

I share this story to show that even some of the small acts of kindness make all the difference in the world for someone who is going through things you had no idea they had going on. Judith healed me without even knowing my affliction. Notably, she healed me without saving me. Judith didn't feel compelled to dive into my life with solutions for all of my struggles. Judith just cared enough to tell me she believed in me. The remainder of the work was mine to do.

This is also a story about seeing beyond the superficial. Everyone has a story that we know nothing about. It is way too easy to make assumptions and judgments about what we see. What lies beneath, however, is where the real story begins.

JOURNAL PROMPT

- Consider a time when someone encouraged or believed in you and it made a difference. Write a letter to that person. Notice how good it feels.

Writing about Your Healing

• • •

've gone to great lengths to point out that healing is so much more than jumping in to fix problems. Healing is about being present, being accepting, being self-aware, and being emotionally connected, and these things are enough.

As you've read this section, do you think you tend to be a helper or a fixer by nature? What impact has this had upon your life? What have you been telling yourself around fixing or healing? What have you been telling others through your actions? What would you like to do to harness that energy into healing?

Reflect a bit on the painful lessons you've experienced in life and how they have shaped you. How do these experiences inform your ability to be a healing presence? What was healing for you?

Consider your inner child, inner parent, and inner adult. Who has control in your life? Do you empower your inner adult to be in control?

What unresolved issues exist in your life that you need to find healing around? What will enhance the healing process for you? What significant things have you healed in the past? How was that able to happen? What steps will you take to facilitate your own healing? What steps will you take to allow others to heal without your intervention?

And a Little (or a Lot of) Gratitude

. . .

I n his fascinating book, *Better: A Surgeon's Notes on Performance*,[22] Dr. Atul Gawande expertly describes what makes people good at their jobs. In a nutshell, Dr. Gawande notes that it is time on task. The more a person does a task, the more skilled a person becomes. Perhaps to instill a sense of self-confidence in writing this book, I made an attempt to estimate just how many hours I have spent listening to stories as a therapist or therapy supervisor. I landed on 15,000 hours as a reasonable minimum (and probably higher if you count supervision and observations).

I mention 15,000 hours to give you an idea of how much professional experience I have hearing about the human experience. There are many times that people consult me and are afraid to share for fear of what I might think. They are riddled with self-doubt, shame, and fear. Knowing this, I will often say, "Keep in mind that there isn't much I haven't heard." But the person on my couch doesn't know this because that person hasn't spent 15,000 hours listening to the intimate details of others' lives.

This is the part that *really* stands out to me. I know that the struggles humans share with me are often secret. In that sense, I feel tremendously privileged and grateful. Listening to these stories has helped me personally know that I am not alone in being a human alongside the rest of you.

I have grown and been healed by all of these stories.

I also deeply know that as part of the human condition, we are so caught up in our own internal experiences and evaluations that we struggle to see beyond them. What we probably never stopped to consider is how we may have helped someone else in simple interactions. We may have changed someone else's life forever just by telling a story, doing a good deed, or sharing a burden.

Each time I sit across from another human being, I am touched.

Approximately twenty-eight years ago, I started working in elementary schools with children. Once, a young boy drew a picture for me following our visit. The picture was a self-portrait, and he drew a wok on his head. The wok had heat waves coming off it. When I asked the boy what this picture meant, he said that I made his head so hot (with thoughts) that he could cook rice on it. This kept me going that year when I was drowning in burnout. I still have the picture, and I look at it from time to time.

I remember an amazing Black man who taught me how some perceive the military to be the only way out of poverty. He shared with me the indescribable pain of serving in war, atrocities witnessed and participated in as part of that service. He taught me about the immeasurable complexities of war, conflict, forgiveness, and bravery. I love this man even though I have not seen him in more than twenty years.

I remember another Black war vet who started drinking when he was six years old as he watched his father die of terminal cancer in the home. As a teen, he wondered if he was gay. He decided to try and drink it away as it was not acceptable in his family or culture. He got sober in our work together and invited me to witness his story at an AA meeting in the inner city at night. I was afraid, but I went, and it transformed my entire being. I also love this man whom I have not seen in more than twenty years.

There are simply too many transformative experiences for me to describe, but here is what I want to highlight. I learned this one, most important lesson of all: *Don't be so quick to judge.*

I know. I know. We have all heard this before. When I said I learned it, I mean I *really* understand it in a profound way.

Judgment seems to be viral in our society, and judgment is malignant. When you spend 15,000 hours listening to real human stories, you learn that life isn't so simple. Sound bites make it easy to *think* you know when you don't know shit. Our minds want to distill extraordinarily complex experiences into simple categories so that we can judge them. This is completely pathological. Nothing in life is simple. As soon as you think it is, know that you have embarked upon a mistaken path.

It is always worth considering, reconsidering, reflecting. This takes time and vulnerability, which are precious and often hard-to-find resources today, but the investment is so worth it.

The awareness of and ability to recognize judgment—both in self and others—is a priceless tool. That is what 15,000 hours of listening has taught me. That is the debt of gratitude I can never pay because I would owe more than I have. This book is my attempt to pay it forward. And even though some people I've met may never have felt like they made a difference, they absolutely have.

In the End

. . .

As you prepare to write, I want you to reflect on what makes you badass. So often, we think it *should* be something monumental, but more so it is the small (not-so-small) things about ourselves and our lives that we've overlooked. Every person reading this book is a survivor. Despite feeling alone, ignored, inadequate, we have survived. Contemplate why.

I propose it's because there is some badass in our stories of grit, growth, hope, and healing. Instead of looking to someone else for inspiration, how about you start with looking at your own life with a little awe and respect? No need to judge. No need to compare.

Just take some time to reflect as if you were on the outside looking in. Be there. Let it sink in. You have survived some serious shit, and it doesn't have to look pretty. Imagine if your story was written by someone else. Wouldn't you find some level of admiration or even inspiration?

I hope you let this be the start of seeing your life through new eyes. We all have chapters in our stories. I encourage you to write your own. Actively think about the story of your life and its most salient lessons.

Life takes grit in order to grow. We grow because of hope, and healing is necessary to do it well.

If, as you read this book, you recognize that you want or need more help, try counseling. I'm clearly biased, but I know that counseling helps if you find the right person for you. Psychologytoday.com is a great website to review the profiles of therapy professionals in your area. You may also try locator.apa.org or helpstartshere.org.

I wish you never-ending grit. I wish you a lifetime of growth. May you always find hope, and may healing be ever-present along the way.

Writing Your Story

. . .

- How do you want to allow yourself to be different after reading this book? What action will you take as a result?
- What are the most important lessons you learned? What stories or messages stood out the most strongly? Why?
- If you could write the story of your own life, what themes about grit, growth, hope, and healing stand out for you?
- What are the already-written chapters in your story, and how has each shaped who you have become?
- What is the title and focus of the next chapter in your life? How will you write it? How will you watch it unfold, and what will you do when things don't go according to plan?

Notes

• • •

1. Rachel Naomi Remen, *Kitchen Table Wisdom: Stories That Heal*, 10th Anniversary Edition (New York: Riverhead Books, 2006).

2. Jack Canfield, Mark Victor Hansen, Amy Newmark, *Chicken Soup for the Soul*, 20th Anniversary Edition (Cos Cob, CT: Chicken Soup for the Soul Publishing, 2013).

3. Brené Brown, *The Call to Courage* (Netflix, 2019).

4. Jodie Eckleberry-Hunt, *Move on Motherf*cker: Live, Laugh & Let Sh*t Go* (Oakland: New Harbinger, 2020).

5. James Pennebaker, *Opening Up by Writing it Down: How Expressive Writing Improves Health and Eases Emotional Pain* (3rd edition) (New York: Guilford Press, 2016).

6. Angela Duckworth, *Grit: The Power of Passion and Perseverance* (New York: Scribner, 2016).

7. Melody Beattie, *Codependent No More: How to Stop Controlling Others and Start Caring for Yourself* (Center City, MN: Hazelden, 1986).

8. Stacy Mosel, "Alcohol Relapse," American Addiction Centers, DrugAbuse.com, updated May 19, 2022, https://drugabuse .com/alcohol-relapse/.

9. Carl G. Jung, *The Collected Works of C. G. Jung, Vol. 7: Two Essays on Analytical Psychology* (Princeton University Press, 1972).

10. *Gaslight,* directed by George Cukor, written by John Van Druten, Walter Reisch, and John L. Balderston, featuring Charles Boyer and Ingrid Bergman (MGM, 1944).

11. Dictionary.com, s.v. "hope (*n.*)," accessed May 24, 2022, https://www.dictionary.com/browse/hope.

12. Jerome Groopman, *The Anatomy of Hope: How People Prevail in the Face of Illness* (New York: Random House, 2005).

13. Benjamin W. Corn, David B. Feldman, and Isaiah Wexler, "The Science of Hope," *Lancet Oncology* 21, no. 9 (September 2020): e452–59, DOI: https://doi.org/10.1016/S1470-2045(20)30210-2.

14. Richard G. Tedeschi et al., *Posttraumatic Growth: Theory, Research, and Applications* (New York: Routledge, 2018).

15. Rachel Naomi Remen, *My Grandfather's Blessings: Stories of Strength, Refuge, and Belonging* (Riverhead Books: New York, 2001).

16. Henry Scott-Holland, "Death Is Nothing at All," taken from *Death Is Nothing at All* (Souvenir Press Ltd., 1987).

17. Shonda Rhimes, *Inventing Anna* (Netflix, 2022).

18. Florence Rush, "The Freudian Coverup," *Feminism and Psychology* 6, no. 2 (May 1996): 260–76, https://doi.org/10.1177/0959353596062015.

19. Eric Berne, *Games People Play: The Basic Handbook of Transactional Analysis* (New York: Vintage, 1964).

20. *A Beautiful Day in the Neighborhood,* directed by Marielle Heller, written by Micah Fitzerman-Blue, Noah Harpster, and Tom Junod, featuring Tom Hanks (Sony Pictures, 2019).

21. John Norcross, *Psychotherapy Relationships That Work: Evidence-based Therapist Responsiveness* (New York: Oxford University Press, 2019).

22. Atul Gawande, *Better: A Surgeon's Notes on Performance* (London: Picador, 2008).

Acknowledgments

· · ·

Thank you to the extraordinary Tina Wainscott for being my cheerleader in chief and to the Turner editorial, marketing, and art teams for incredible support and encouragement.

Most importantly, thank you to every person who has inspired me with personal stories of grit, growth, hope, and healing. My work remains an incredible privilege.

Finally, thank you, Judith. Teachers are unsung heroes who often don't ever hear future chapters in the lives of students. You changed my life.

About the Author

· · ·

JODIE ECKLEBERRY-HUNT, PHD, ABPP, is a board-certified health psychologist and executive coach. She lives in Michigan with her husband, two sons, and family treasure, Bacon.